WW2 Letters Home From The South Pacific

ANGELO BUCCINO

WW2 Letters Home From The South Pacific
By Angelo Buccino

ISBN-13: 9781729270219

Published by
Cherry Blossom Press
PO Box 110252
NUTLEY NJ 07110

V 1.00

August 26, 2019

This one's for you, Papa...
I miss you, as do we all.
Stay safe, and eat lots of Trout!
I remember cast iron pans with the
tail turned up! **DEDICATION** Thank you for
the first
a Billion
years!

Thank you for the first a Billion years! ♡

Behrins

Thank you, Pfc. Angelo M. Buccino,
for the years you spent overseas
away from your family
to preserve our freedom.

Thank you, Mitch Mosior
for preserving these letters
in your long-forgotten footlocker.

ACKNOWLEDGMENTS

Mitch and Helen Mosior
Mary Ellen and Ronn Merritt
Marie Cocozza Buccino
Dawn and Andrea Buccino

National Personnel Records Center
Anthony 'Andy' Andriola, Nelson Rummel,
Russell Roemmele, Ed Stecewicz,
Ruth Robertson, Gus Vaccaro

Thank you, Veterans

CONTENTS

FOREWORD

On November 16, 1918, Angelo was born to Lucia and Domenick Buccino on Columbia Avenue in Nutley, N.J. He joined siblings Assunta, Costanza, Giuseppe and Palma. The family later moved to Passaic Avenue, then Gless Avenue, both in Belleville. Domenick, a vegetable peddler, died in 1929, leaving Lucy with two houses on Gless Avenue and a large garden where she grew most of what the family ate.

Angelo enjoyed life on the dead end cobblestone street and attended School Seven with friends, siblings and other relatives who lived in the neighborhood. In the farm like neighborhood, the family had goats, chickens and dogs, too. Growing up, Angelo and his best friend and neighbor Mitch and his brothers, enjoyed raising and racing homing pigeons.

When the Depression came along, Angelo entered the Civilian Conservation Corps., a public work relief program for unemployed, unmarried men. There he learned carpentry skills which would come in handy building redoubts on various islands in the South Pacific.

Angelo M. Buccino entered the U.S. Army on February 7, 1941. He served with Americal division with the First Marine Division, Reinforced, on Guadalcanal the Fiji Islands and unnamed places in the South Pacific. He was honorably discharged on September 22, 1945.

On July 12, 1973, a huge fire at the National Personnel Records Center in St. Louis, destroyed approximately 18 million Official Military Personnel Files. Buccino's records were among those lost. However, the letters here tell a very small part of his encounters during the war.

In 2003, upon the passing of Mitch and Helen Mosior several months apart, a WW2 era footlocker was discovered in their attic. Inside were letters written to Mitch by his friends before and early in his deployment in WW2. Among those letters to Mitch and Hellen were 19 letters home from the South Pacific by Angelo Buccino.

DRAFTED, IN THE ARMY NOW

Angelo M. Buccino entered the U.S. Army on February 7, 1941

2 PANAMA CANAL

April 25, 1942

Hello Met,

It's been a long time since I wrote hasn't it. Well how are you feeling these days. Begin training pigeons yet? Here's hoping you walk off with a few races in Young Birds. Sorry I couldn't see your loft last time I was home but I had a lot of things to do & only had one day to do it. You know the way it is when you're looking the birds over. Time sure flies. I wish I had a few pair here. I saw some of the pigeons they have in Australia. I only saw them from the sidewalk, so I can't tell you much about them. If I'm lucky to return & stop back there I'll try bringing some home.

We left N.Y. a few days after you saw me and our voyage was on. We left N.Y. with a helluva cold spell & 4 days later we were stripped and taking Sun Baths. Going through Panama Canal was very interesting as I was always in the dark as to how the locks worked. This was the first chance we've had to mail letters, they were all censored, just as all our mail is.

Feb. 7th my one year was up and my girlfriend wrote & told me it was the same cold rainy weather as when I left. It was raining as we left the armory & we passed Charley's Washing Machine shop. I hollered across the street to him & he waved back. Next time you see him ask him if he still remembers. Then at Dix we got soaked walking from the train to our tents – that leaked like Eugene's pigeon coop (your kid brother). Ha ha. I almost landed in the same place again as we moved from Virginia to Dix. About 2 blocks away this time and again rain rain rain.

We kept sailing along, no one knows where we are going. So now I know how Columbus felt, sailing on & on, no one knowing where to. Then one day we got word we were Australia bound & we hit rough weather. I was sicker than a dog, the ships were going up & down and water was coming on deck. It felt good to set foot on dry land – "just once more." (As I kept wishing all thru the trip.) In Australia we had a good time and were treated to the best Hospitality I've ever seen. But all this was too good to last and orders came through to sail again.

A few weeks later we land on an island called New Caledonia (betcha can't find it) in the Pacific. Up until now we haven't been able to mention where we are but the ban has been lifted. We are far from town, Met and it's every once in a while you're able to go. I personally don't care to go as there isn't anything there anyway. The way I feel the next time I want to see the town is homeward bound.

We haven't the things here we had back in America. But we are getting used to conditions and learning ways to getting around them. I have some candy made by Charms Inc. in Bloomfield, as soon as I got the can, I wished I could be at the shop where it was made. We have a combination radio phonograph and along with it is about 150 records. I eat my heart out as I listen to them as they bring back memories of Better Days. But it's a good way to be reminded of back home.

Since we came here we worked in rain & heat. We got our positions up & everything's coming along fine. The rainy season is on here and never a day goes by without us getting rain. One day last week we got a taste of what to expect when a real Tropical storm comes along. It rained 5 days straight without stopping. It's a good thing we have 8 sets of clothes.

There are few white people here, mostly natives and French Javanese. There are a lot of coconuts, oranges and bananas about the Island. What I hate about this place is the mosquitoes & ants. I wish I had taken up French in school, as I would be able to talk to the people here. That's another reason I stick around the camp. This is jungle country and it reminds me of the Tarzan pictures I used to see.

In spite of the heat, I'm feeling all right. And when I listen to an American broadcast, I feel even better, man my heart skips a few beats. From what I've seen, if I ever get back to America, I'll be like that guy hopping the Chattanooga Choo Choo. I'll never roam any more. There's nothing like the States. Met, take it from me. I can't understand why people spent money to go to Europe when there was so much to see in the States. Yeah man it's beyond me.

Your probably wondering when I'll be home. Well I can't say but with a prayer, and a little luck, I hope to be home Christmas. This is my opinion and I may be well be here for over a year. (Pardon me I just knocked on wood.) So Chet tied the knot eh! It sure was a surprise to hear about it from Sub (??) and my brother. Bruno was even a bigger surprise!

Marie tells me she mistook the draft list for the Radio Column. Its two full rows and they've just about cleaned out the 1st Ward in Newark. She also said you'd practically have to be a corpse to be rejected. I let Bernie Barnett know a thing like being rejected for teeth would never keep us out of the Army if War was declared. So I'm glad I came in when I did as I stand a 50 – 50 chance this way.

Does Bruno still get to Vuono's for a few with Charlie. How's the boys getting along. I heard a few joined the Navy. Pretty soon more will get drafted and good bye the ole gang!

Well Met, the sooner we get this mess over & done with the sooner we'll all get together. I met some fellows from Nutley about 3 weeks ago. Imagine meeting somebody you know from back home, way out here. There's about 21 hours difference in time, we're that much ahead of you.

Well Met, I think I'll close asking you to give my regards to the gang (what's left of them). And tell (ink stain) her. A lot of times the boys (ink stain) my mind & I wonder where they are and how they're doing. But I hope we all meet again, someday and will celebrate.

So long Met, name a bird after me. He'll come thru. "Keep em Flying Kid."

Regards to the Gang and Family

Angelo

PS Did Charlie McIntyre leave for the Army yet? Ask his brother George next time you see him & also give him my regards!

How's Boom Boom (your sister) She's getting Fat I think!

Pfc. Angelo Buccino
244th CA. Bty 7 - 6814+
A.P.O. 502
C/o Postmaster
San Francisco, Calif.

April 25, 1942

Hello Met,

Its been a long time since I wrote, hasnt it? Well how are you feeling these days, begun training the Pigeons yet? Heres hoping you walk off with a few races in Young Birds. Sorry I couldn't see your loft last time I was home but I had a lot of things to do & I only had one day to do it. You know the way it is when you start looking the birds over. I'm sure this. I wish I had a few pair here I saw some of the pigeons they have in Australia. I only saw them from the sidewalk, so I can't tell you much about them! If I'm lucky to return & stop back there I'll try bringing some home.

We left N.Y. a few days after you saw me and our voyage was on. We left N.Y. with a billive cold spell & 4 days later we were stripped and taking Sun Baths. Going thru Panama Canal was very interesting as I was always in the dark as to how the locks worked. This was the first chance we had to mail letters, they were all censored, just as all our mail is.

Feb 1st, my one year was up and my girlfriend wrote & told me it was the same cold rainy weather as I left. It was raining as we left the Armory & we passed Charley's Washing Machine shop. I hollered across the street to him & he waved back. Next time you all him ask him if he still remembers. Then at Dix we got soaked walking from the train to our tents. That looked like Eugenes pigeon corp (your kid brother). Ha.Ha. Jelmont landed in the same place again as we moved from Virginia to Dix. About 2 blocks away this time and again Rain Rain Rain.

We kept sailing along, no one knew where we were going, to
now I know how Columbus over felt, sailing on & on, no one
knowing where to. Then one day we were in were Australia
bound & we hit rough weather. I was sicker than a dog, the
ships were going up & down and water was coming on deck.
But finally Australia were sighted. We landed all right and
it felt good to set foot on dry land - just one more. (So I kept
wishing all the ~~time~~) In Australia we had a good time
& were treated to the best hospitality I've ever seen. But all this
~~it's~~ too good to last and orders came thru to sail again.
A few weeks later we land on an Island called New Caledonia
(betcha you can't find it) in the Pacific. Up until now we haven't
been able to mention where we are but the ban has been lifted.
We are far from town, meat and etc every once in a while you
able to go. I personally don't care to go as there isn't anything
there anyway. The way I feel the next time down ~~~~ ~~~~
~~~~ is Homeward bound.

We haven't the things here that we had back in America
But we are getting used to conditions and learning of ways to
getting around when. I have some candy made by Thurm's Inc
in Bloomfield, as soon as I got the can. I wished I could be at
the shop where it was made. We have a combination radio-
phonograph and along with it is about 150 records. It eats
my heart out as I listen to them as they bring back memories
of Better Days. But its a good way to be reminded of back
home.

Since we came here we worked, rain & heat. We got
our positions up & everything coming along fine. The rainy
season is on here and never a day goes by without us getting
rain. One day last week we got a taste of what to expect
when a real Tropical storm comes along. It rained 5 days
straight without stopping. Its a good thing we have 8 sets of clothes

There are few white people here, mostly natives + French Javanese. There are a lot of coconuts, oranges, + bananas about the Island. What I hate about this place is the mosquitoes & ants. I wish I had taken my lunch in school, as I would be able to talk to the people here. That's another reason I stick around the Camp. This is jungle country + it reminds me of the Tarzan pictures I used to see.

In spite of the [illegible], I'm feeling all right. And when I listen to an American Broadcast, I feel even better, man my chips a few beats. From what I've seen, if I ever get back to America, I'll be like that guy hopping the Chattanooga Choo Choo. I'll never roam any more. There's nothing like the States Met, take it from me. I can't understand why people spent money to go to Europe when there was so much to see in the States. Yeah man it's beyond me.

You're probably wondering when I'll be home. Well I can't say but with a prayer, and a little luck, I hope to be home Christmas. This is my opinion and it may be will be here for over a year (Pardon me I just knocked on wood). So Chet tied the knot eh! It sure was a surprise to hear about it from Sut and my brother. Bruno was a bigger surprise!

Marie tells me she mistook the draft list for the Radio Column. It's two full rows and they've just about cleaned out the 1st ward in Newark. She also said you'd practically have to be a corpse to be rejected. I like Bernie Barnett [illegible] a thing like being rejected for teeth would never keep us out of the Army if War was declared. So I'm glad I came in when I did as I stand a 50-50 chance this way.

Does Bruno still go to Nunos for a few with Charlie. How the boys getting along. I heard a few joined the Navy. Pretty soon some more will be drafted and good bye the old gang!

8

Well Mat, the sooner we get this mess over & done with the sooner we'll all get together. I met some fellows from Nutley about 3 weeks ago. Imagine meeting somebody you know from back home, way out here. There's about 21 hours difference in time, were that much ahead of you.

Well Mat I think I'll close asking you to give my regards to the ▓▓▓▓ (whats left of them), and tell the ▓▓▓▓▓▓▓▓▓▓ her. A lot of times the boys ▓▓ in my mind & I wonder where they are and how they're doing. But I hope we all meet again, someday and will celebrate.

So long Mat, name a bird after me. Hell, come over here. "Keep em flying Kid."

Regards to the Gang

& family.

Angelo

P.S. Did Charlie M. Intyre leave for the army yet? Ask his brother George next time you see him & also give him my regards.

Have Boom Boom (your sister) She getting fat I think!

3 FORTY FRENCH WORDS

Sept. 26, 1942

Hi There Metalski,

I just received your letter of August 24th and I was glad too. We must have made a good connection that time as letters generally take 1 to 2 months to reach here.

Yes the Marines sure had a field day knocking them Japs out of the sky. This time the Japs were caught with their pants down. There's fighting going on there now but I haven't listened to a radio for over a week, so I don't know how things are up there.

I heard about the send off Val got & I also heard that he's in Washington now. They sure shipped him fast & far. That's the second time he's been to the West Coast. Well Met maybe when this reaches you you'll be in the Service also. It seems like every guy & his brother are in uniform these days.

So you're the Uncle to Judith Ann Mosior Eh? How does it feel. I've been an Uncle since I was two years old. My niece was married in April and her husband is in the Service too. So your engaged Met, well whatever you do don't get married before or while you're in the Service. They say it's much easier to leave a girlfriend behind than a wife. I guess they're right too. Wish you luck in getting into the Air Corps. Let me know how Chet makes out.

So Butchie came through and got 7th in the Club. Well he'll get his stride & bring home the bacon yet. Well you got 1st place in the other club so it ain't so bad is it?

Well Met all you said about Love & your girlfriend there isn't much that

I can add except – Check! – Wish you luck in your affair. The jokes you wrote were good. I didn't hear them.

That's a date Met and we'll drink a toast when the introduction takes place. Don't build me up too much as she may be a little disappointed in what she sees. I said Maybe!

No Met I don't use the sign language on French girls instead I've bought a few books for beginners & now my vocabulary is about 40 words. Slow but sure. Honest Met you say hello to some of them & and they'll smile and answer you but some will stick up their nose as if they were the last woman God created. I never saw such a crazy bunch of gals in my life.

Your dam right, them Japs better stay the hell away from here if they ever want to see Tokyo or Yokohama again. We've been on this island a long time & all we've done is build & build and practice and what the hell not. We're ready anytime.

Thanks kid for saying a prayer for me. Up until a few weeks ago I used to attend church practically every Sunday but now – well something happened and I don' go. They say there are no Atheists in Fox holes. They're right there ain't.

Well kid I like your letters because they're nice and long and the dope it contains, so keep writing don't wait for an answer as then it will be a lot of time wasted for waiting. I'll do likewise Met. I'm sure you'll find it better this way. I'll write at least twice a month.

We are busy working, which isn't unusual to us anymore. But that's alright as it occupies your mind. Our soft ball has been cut out for a while to as we often work the whole seven days.

I was on a detail in town for two weeks and I worked in a ship. It reminded of better times back home punching the time clock again. I saw a lot of the town in those two weeks. Yeah Man!

I guess I'll close now and glad to hear your using sense in waiting for this mess to be over before getting married. I heard from my brother Val who is Ireland. He's a corporal now. But like us, we wish we were back in the good ole U.S.A. Yes we've learned to appreciate all the luxury & things of home. You don't miss em much until you have to do without it. So long now Met. Wish you luck in the Races, Air Corps, & with your girlfriend. Remember me to your friend (Butch!)

Angelo

P.S. Write my address plainer Met as the Battery F was underlined in red for not being plain enough. (maybe he needs glasses as I can read it plain enough.)

P.F.C. Angelo Buccino
244th C.A. Bty 7
A.P.O. 502
C/o Postmaster
San Francisco, Calif
Sept. 26, 1942

Hi there Mitalski,

I just received your letter of August 24th and I was glad too. We must have made a good connection that time as letters generally take 1 to 2 months to reach here.

Yes the marines sure had a field day knocking them Japs out of the sky. This time the Japs were caught with their pants down. There's fighting going on there now but I haven't listened to a radio for over a week, so I don't know how things are up there

I heard about the send off Val got I also heard that he is in Washington now. They sure shipped him fast & far. That's the second time he's been to the west coast. Well Mit maybe when this reaches you you'll be in the service also. It seems like every guy & his brother are in uniform these days.

So your the Uncle to Judith Ann Moison eh? How does it feel. I've been an Uncle since I was two years old. My niece was married in April

and her husband is in the Service too. So
you're engaged Mat, well whatever you do don't
get married before or while your in the Service.
They say its much easier to leave a girlfriend behind
than a wife. I guess they're right too. Wish you luck
in getting into the Air Corps. Let me know how that
makes out.

So Butchie came thru and got 7th in the Clist
well he'll get his stride & bring home the bacon yet.
Well you got 1st place in the other Club so it ain't so
bad is it?

Well Mat all you said about Love + your girlfriend
there ain't much that I can add except -- Chick !--
Wish you luck in your affair. The jokes you
wrote were good, didn't hear them.

Thats a date Mat and we'll drink a toast when
the introduction takes place. Don't build me up too
much as she may be a little disappointed in what
she saw. I said maybe!

No Mat I don't use the sign language on

French gals instead I've bought a few books for
beginners & now my vocabulary is about 40
words. Slow but sure. Aren't that you say
hello to some of them & they'll smile & answer you
but some will stick up their nose as if they were
the last women God created. I never saw such a
bunch of crazy gals in my life.

Your dam right, them Japs better stay the
hell away from here if they ever want to see
Tokyo or Yokohama again. We've been on this island
a long time & all we've done is build & build, practice
and what the hell not. We're ready anytime.

Thanks kid for saying a prayer for me. Up until
a few weeks ago I used to attend Church practically every
Sunday but now — — well something happened and I
don't go. They say there are no Atheists in Fox holes.
They're right there ain't.

Well kid I like your letters because they're nice
and long and the dope it contains, so keep writing
don't wait for an answer as then it will be a lot

(P.S. Write my address plainer Met as) (maybe be nade)
the Betting 7 was underlined in) (plainer as I can)
Red for not being plain enough. (read it plain enough.)

of time wasted for waiting. I'll do likewise Met.
I'm sure you'll find it better this way. I'll write
at least twice a month.

We are busy working, which isn't unusual
to us anymore. But thats alright as it occupies
your mind. Our soft ball has been cut out for awhile
too so we often work the whole seven days.

I was on a detail in town for two weeks and
I worked in a shop. It reminded of better times back
home punching the time clock again. I saw a lot
of the town in those two weeks. Jot Man!

I guess I'll close now and glad to hear your
using sense in waiting for this mess to be
over before getting married. I heard from my cousin
Val who is in Ireland. He's a Cpl now. But like
us, we wish we were back in the good old U.S.G.
Yes were learned to appreciate all the luxurys + things
of home. You don't miss em Much until you have to
do without it. So long now Met. Wish you luck
in the Ross, his Cage, + with your girlfriend. Remember me to
her. Thanks.
                                    Your friend (Dutch)
                                         Angelo

4 MITCHELL 2000

October 4, 1942

Hello Met, alias "Mitchell 2000"

Just a few lines to let you know I'm alright and hope you're feeling the same. How are you and the girlfriend getting along? Fine I hope. It was a surprise to me learning you were going steady. You never did care for women much anyway. But when she came along well your resistance was low, eh? They're all bound to fall some day no matter how much they dislike women.

How's Mike Siluk, I wrote to him several times but only got one answer and that was four months ago. Say Met have you ever seen Toot Bloomenshine around? How's Joe Metz, Charlie Chas, Metty, Silver Top (Chet's brother Johnny), Skippy & John Nuriki? I guess a lot of those guys are not around town anymore.

I'm sending you a snapshot of myself that I had taken several weeks ago. I thought you would like to have one being I have one of you & the girlfriend.

There's nothing much I can say about things here Met, but were busy as hell. We've had the past two Sundays off & a few guys got up a ball game. The weather is cool & windy, it keeps the mosquitoes inland. When we first landed here, they practically ate us alive. I've never seen them as thick as they are here. We have several boys in our outfit who come from Florida & they say the mosquitoes down at the "Keys" are much worse than these. The Natives don't seem to be bothered much by them.

Maybe they prefer white meat.

My girlfriend mentioned a clipping she saw in the paper a few months ago. It was about a girl writing to her boyfriend in Australia asking, "What have they got that we haven't." He answered, "Oh nothing, except they're over here." I don't think she could think of an answer to that. But let me tell you Met I spent a week in Australia, yes they have their pretty women and all that but the American girls got it all over them as far as knowledge & being hip to the jive.

There are a lot of marriages taking place wherever Yanks are stationed. But that's the way it goes and I can't say as I blame them. But here's one guy that's coming home single, you can bet your last dollar on that. That is, if I come back at all, you know nothing is certain nowadays.

Today is Sunday & I go on guard duty tonight. We get a lot of that as we're {content cut from paper}. They'll never catch us napping Met. I don't know how the war is going except for what I read on the Bulletin board. But I hope to be home in the Spring or early Summer. But who knows?

There's about eight guys here in my outfit that come from Jersey, but most of them come from N.Y. and Tennessee. I haven't heard from Val as yet but I did get a letter about four days ago, but it was written Aug. 16th that was before he left for the Army.

Well Met I guess I'll be moving along now as I have a few more letters to write. I'll write again soon. Hoping this letter finds you all well and in the best of health. Give the Gang my regards and tell them to write.

So long

Your friend Angelo

P.F.C. Angelo Buccino
244 th C.A. Bty 7
A.P.O. 502
% Postmaster
San Francisco Calif.
Oct. 4, 1942

Hello Met & "Mitchell 2000"

Just a few lines to let you know I'm alright and I hope your feeling the same. How are you and the girlfriend getting along? Fine I hope. It was a surprise to me hearing you were going steady, you never did care for women much anyway. But when she came along well your resistance was low eh? They're all bound to fall someday no matter how much they dislike women.

Have Mike Siluk, I wrote to him several times but only got one answer and that was about four months ago. Say Met have you ever seen Fort Blumenstine around? Have Joe Metz, Charlie Chas, Matty, Sebu Syp (Chito brother Johnny), Skippy & John Yurski? I guess maybe a lot of these guys are not around town anymore.

I'm sending you a snapshot of myself that I had taken several weeks ago. I thought you would like to have me being I have one of you & the girlfriend.

There's nothing much I can say about things here Met, but were busy as hell. We've had the past two Sundays off & a few guys got up a ball game. The weather is cool & windy, It keeps the mosquitos inland. When we first landed here, they practically ate us alive, I've never seen them as thick as they are here. We have several boys in our outfit who came from Florida & they say the mosquitos down at the "Keys" are much worse than these. The natives don't seem to be bothered much by them.

Maybe they prefer white meat.

My girlfriend mentioned a clipping she saw in the paper a few months ago. It was about a girl writing to her boyfriend in Australia asking, "what have they got that we haven't". He answered, "It's nothing, except that they're over here". I don't think she could think of an answer to that. But let me tell you that 2 spent a week in Australia, yes they have their pretty women and all that but our American girls got it all over them as far as knowledge & being hip to the jive.

Sure there are a lot of marriages taking place wherever yanks are stationed. But that's the way it goes and I can't say as I blame them. But here's the guy that's coming home single, you can bet your last dollar on that. That is if I come back at all, you know nothing is certain nowadays.

Today is Sunday & I go on guard duty tonight. We get a lot of that over _____ They'll never catch me napping Milt. I don't know how the are going to let up for ____ I read in the Bulletin head. But I hope to be home in the spring or early summer. But who knows?

There's about eight guys here in our outfit that come from Jersey, but most of them come from Jersey & Tennessee. I haven't heard from Val as yet but I did get a letter about four days ago but it was written Aug 16th & that was before he left for the army.

Well Milt, I guess I'll be moving along now as I have a few more letters to write. I'll write again soon. Hoping this letter finds you all well & in the best of health. My regards to all then to write. Say the Gang. Your friend Vincent.

5 BEST FRIEND: RIFLE

Oct. 16, 1942

Hello Met,

How are you Mitchell 2000? How's the girlfriend too? I wrote to you about two weeks ago & sent along a snapshot that I thought you'd like to have. Have you received it?

Well, how did "Pigeon Dealer Tiny" train the birds? In fact how did the Young Birds Series turn out? Racing in two clubs sure must increase the excitement on Sundays, eh? Did Butchie do any better later in the races? I stopped in to see some birds that the Army has here and it was just like ole times back home. Seeing them birds was sight for sore eyes.

Boy its getting hot here & it isn't even summer time yet. It's just the opposite of back home. We're still busy working on that project and in two months we should finish up.

Say Met I didn't know Muzz was in the Navy? How did Chet make out in trying for the Air Corps.? You have the same ideas eh? You know Tiny would stand a good chance being he's a licensed mechanic already. But I guess he's satisfied working at the Airport. Tell that guy Suhe (Mike) to leave the women alone for half hour and drop me a line. This guy Andy that stays with Charlie, is he in the Army yet? He was one of the first to go from the street but I guess I beat them all getting in. How the heck do you spell Charlie's last name? Micheski? Dolly tells me she's going out with Shum. The lucky stiff.

No kidding Met but it's good to hear what's going on back home ...

news about the old gang etc. Boy we're going to have some celebration when we get back. Met get me the addresses of Alex & Billy Duduck, Muzz any of the ole gang that you can. I'd like to drop them a line. Do you know any of the ships they're on?

How's that big fellow Eugene, does he drive your car? Boom Boom is still having his legs run off eh? She was a regular Fatstuff when I last seen her. Just wait till she gets a gander at this Fat Guy, 176 pounds Met. She'll have the laugh on me.

Well Met I haven't got anything else to say right now but I'll be back in a few weeks with another letter. I hope this reaches you before Christmas. I just remembered I have to clean my rifle as I was on guard duty yesterday. In the Army your rifle is your best friend, treat it well.

So long now Met look up the addresses to them guys & let me have them. Give my brother Val my regards in your next letter. Keep em flying kid. Give the gang my regards.

Your friend
Angelo

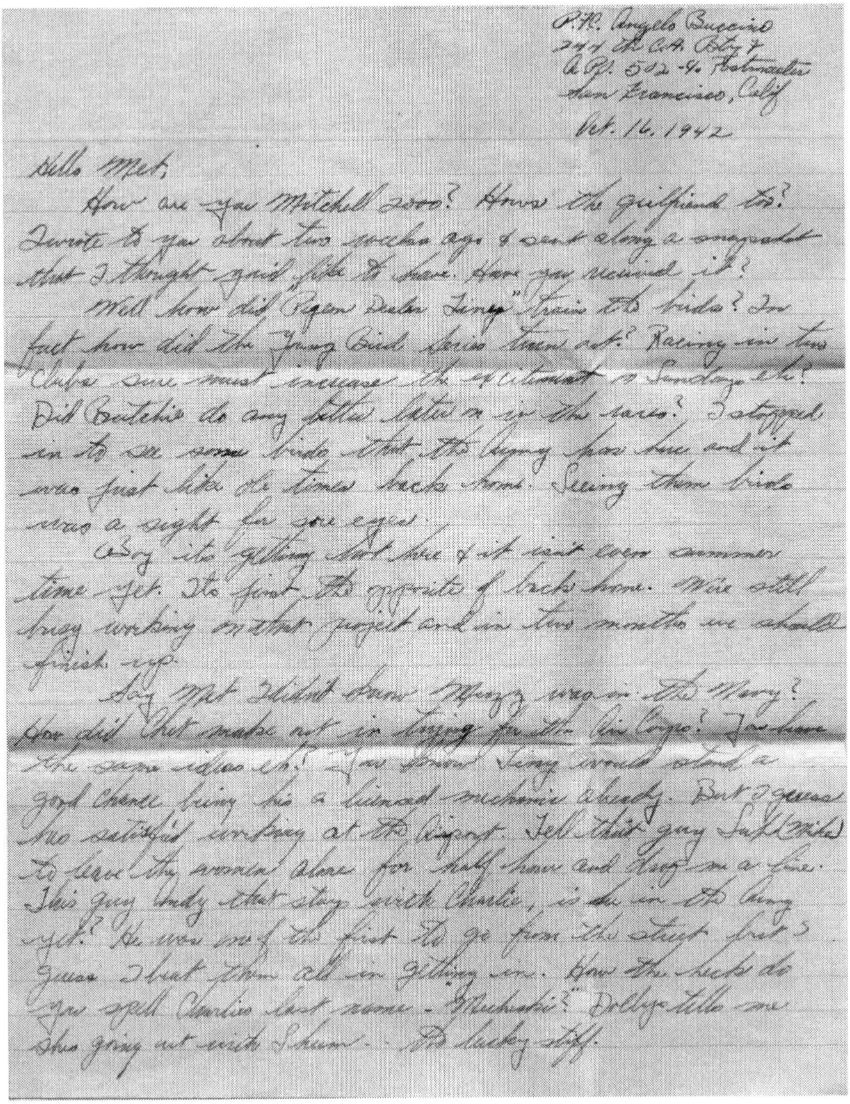

P.F.C. Angelo Buccino
[illegible service address]
A.P.O. 502 ℅ Postmaster
San Francisco, Calif.

Oct. 16, 1942

Hello Mit;

How are you Mitchell avoo? Hows the girlfriend too? I wrote to you about two weeks ago & sent along a snapshot that I thought you'd like to have. Have you received it?

Well how did "Pigeon Dealer Timy" train the birds? In fact how did the Young Bird Series turn out? Racing in two clubs sure must increase the excitement on Sunday eh? Did Butchie do any better latter on in the races? I stopped in to see some birds that the army has here and it was just like the times back home. Seeing them birds was a sight for sore eyes.

Boy its getting hot here & it isn't even summer time yet. Its just the opposite of back home. We're still busy working on that project and in two months we should finish up.

Say Mit I didn't know Muzzy was in the Navy? How did Art make out in trying for the Air Corps? You have the same idea eh? You know Timy would stand a good chance being he a licensed mechanic already. But I guess hes satisfied working at the Airport. Tell that guy Safe Side to leave the women alone for half hour and drop me a line. This guy Woody that stay with Charlie, is he in the army yet? He was one of the first to go from the street first I guess I beat them all in getting in. How the heck do you spell Charlie last name - Michicki? Dollye tells me shes going out with Schum - the lucky stiff.

in building Mat but its good to hear whats going on
back home... news about the ole gang etc. Boy we're going
to have some celebration when we get back. Mat get me
the address of Alex & Billy Duduck, though any of the ole gang
that you can. I'd like to drop them a line. Do you know
any of the ships they're on?

How's that big fellow Eugene, does he drive your car!
Dom Bom is still having his legs run off eh? He was
a regular Falstaff when I last saw him. Just wait till he
gets a gander at this fat guy, 176 pounds Mat. He'll
have the laugh on me.

Well Mat I haven't got anything else to say right
now but I'll be back in a few weeks with another letter.
I hope this reaches you before Christmas. I just remembered I
have to clean my rifle as I was on guard duty yesterday.
In the army your rifle is your best friend, treat it well.

So long now Mat look up the address to those guys
& let me have them. Give my brother Val my regards in
your next letter. Keep em flying eh! Give the gang
my regards.

Your friend

Angelo

6 GUADALCANAL

Nov. 4, 1942

Hello Met,

It's been a long time since I last wrote to you but it couldn't be helped. Notice my new address Met & always include my serial number when you write.

I am stationed at Guadalcanal & that's just about all I'm allowed to say. But you'll get the news flashes over the radio & in newspapers.

I sent a shell with "Regards from Met" in it across the lines. I hope it hit some Japs. Since I've been here I met some guys from Jersey & boy they're from all over Jersey.

I am feeling fine these days & really feel good that I'm in it at last. We haven't much time to ourselves anymore and I find little time to write.

Well before this reaches you, you may be in uniform also. Well anyone can read this letter in your family & then send it on to you wherever your stationed. Tell Charlie Milsreski where I am, will you?

How's Bruno, wife & baby coming along. I hope to see more than one when I come back Bruno or I'll think you're slipping. Has Eugene joined the Navy? I hear Tiny is in the Air Corp. What's happened to Charlie (Julius) I haven't heard about him except he got a new job and questionnaire. Tell Mike Siluk to write & to expect a letter one of these days.

I can just picture that street in a deserted condition. Well our street put a lot of guys in the Service. That's what I like to hear.

I'll close now with Regards to everybody in your family & the gang. (What's left of them).

So long Met

Your friend Butch

Ange

Angelo Barcino - 32059032
Marine Corp. Unit 900
% Postmaster
San Francisco, Calif.
Nov. 4, 1942

Hello Mel,

It's been a long time since I last wrote to you but it couldn't be helped. Notice my new address Mel + always include my serial number (32059032) when you write.

I am stationed at Guadalcanal + that's just about all I'm allowed to say. But you'll get the news flashes over the radio + in newspapers.

I sent a shell with - "Regards from Mel" in it across the lines. I hope it hit some Japs. Since I've been here I met some guys from Jersey + boy they're from all over Jersey.

I am feeling fine these days + really feel good that I'm in it at last. We haven't much time to ourselves anymore and I find little time to write.

Well before this reaches you, you may
be in uniform also. Will anyone
ever read this letter in your family & then
send it on to you wherever you stationed.
Tell Charlie Mizeski where I am, will you?

How Bruno, wife & baby coming along.
I hope to see more than one when I come
back Bruno or I'll think you're slipping.
Has Eugene joined the Navy? Has Tiny is
in the Air Corp. What happened to Charlie
(Julius) I haven't heard about him ~~+ yet~~
he got a new job & questionaire. Tell Mike
Siluk to write & I'd expect a letter one
of these days.

I can just picture that street in
a deserted condition. Well no street
put a lot of guys in the service. That's
what I do it man.

I'll close now with regards to everybody in your family & the gang. (What's
left of them). So long Matt
Your friend Butch
Ange.

7 ZERO BRACELET

Nov. 28, 1942

Hello Metalski,

I just received your letter of Oct. 25th I was glad to hear the dope. Yes I guess this letter will be forwarded to you wherever your stationed. I wrote to you a few days ago Met but just had to write again & answer your letter.

So my brother got married eh, well I wish him luck. Let me know your address as soon as possible Tiny, Eugene & Charley too.

Met I have moved from that other place & I can't reveal my new location anymore. Ask your sister to get any letters I wrote to her in November and you'll know where I am. Were in action at last Met & I wrote your name on shells and sent them over the lines into Japs laps. I'd like to write about a lot of things Met but I just can't.

I have a few souvenirs socked away – Jap money, dope & parts of Zero fighters. I made a bracelet for my girl from the fuselage of a Zero that was shot down near here.

I just came back from a swim in the water & I feel like a million bucks. I washed some clothes too. I took a picture of myself naked & I will show it to you if it comes out. You'll have to wait until I get home though. (By next Christmas I hope!) Well it's ten months overseas for this boy. I'm used to this heat & everything I've found in the tropics. It's much hotter here being we're near the equator.

I met some Marines from Kearny & Newark, so it's a small world after all.

So Belleville hasn't been defeated in football, let me know if they remained undefeated. It seems they always outplay their opponents but always end up in a tie or lose. At least that's the way it was when I was going to high school anyway.

I guess Helen was tickled pink when you placed that ring on her finger, eh? I keep telling my girl I'm not going to buy her any engagement ring, but I am. Of course all this is subject to change without notice. But so far those Japs haven't drawn a bead on this boy.

So you were to Radio City, well I never was there myself but am I going to make up for lost time when I get back. You never know how lucky you were where there was everything until you land in a place like this where there isn't anything. I often say to myself how foolish I was for not seeing more of life while I was able. But being back home you figure heck there's plenty of time.

Heck it's about time the Yankees lost for the interest of baseball itself. I don't think anyone wants to see any one team win year after year. It gets monotonous eh kid.

You were more fortunate than I am having your girlfriend beside you & having her (censor?) it. Oh boy would I like to have been in your shoes but with my girlfriend. No offense Met. You understand & besides I wouldn't try cutting in on you.

I guess I'll close stations now Metalski. I'm feeling fine & glad to hear your niece is coming around. Let me have Bruno's address

Your friend, Ange

I wish you a Merry Christmas And A Happy New Year.

Please forward this to Met if he's in the Army or Navy. Regards to all

P.F.C. Angelo Buccino 32059032
Marine Corps Unit 900
c/o Postmaster
San Francisco, Calif.
November 28, 1942

Hello Matteski;

I just received your letter of Oct. 25th
& was glad to hear the dope. Yes I
guess this letter will be forwarded
to you wherever your stationed. I
wrote to you a few days ago Matt
but just had to write again &
answer your letter.

So my brother got married eh,
well I wish him luck. Let me
know Jan address as soon as possible
Tiny, Eugene & Charley too.

Matt I have moved from that
other place & I can't reveal my
new location anymore. Ask John
sister to get any letter I wrote to
my mother in November & you'll know
where I am. When in action at last
Matt & I wrote you nine or ten

& sent them over the lines into Jap laps. I like to write about a lot of things yet but I just can't.

I have a few souvenirs socked away - Jap money, dope & parts of Zero fighters. I made a bracelet for my girl from the fuselage of a Zero that was shot down near here.

I just came back from a swim in the river & I feel like a million bucks. I washed some clothes too. I took a picture of myself all naked & I will show it to you if it comes out. You'll have to wait until I get home though. (By next Christmas I hope.)

Well its ten months overseas for this boy. I'm used to this heat & everything else found in the tropics. Its much hotter here being we're nearer to the equator.

I met some Marines from Kearny & Newark, so its a small world after all.

So Belleville hasn't been defeated in football, let me know if they remain undefeated. It seems they always out play their opponits but always end up in a tie or lose. At least that the way it was when I was going to high school anyway.

I guess Helen was tickled pink when you placed that ring on her finger eh? I keep telling you girl I'm not going to buy her any engagement ring, but I am. Of course all this is subject to change without notice. But so far those Japs haven't drawn a bead on this boy.

So you were to Radio City, well I never was there myself but am I going to make up for lost time when I get back. You never know how

I wish you all a Merry Christmas And a Happy New Year.

Please forward this to rest of fellows in the Armory Mary. Regards Bill.

Lucky you were when there was everything until you land in a place like this when there isn't anything. Often say to myself how foolish I was for not seeing more of life while I was able. But being back home you figure back these [slips] of time.

Heck its about time the Yankees lost for the interest of baseball itself. Dont think anyone wants to see any one team win year after year. It gets monotonous eh Sal.

You were more fortunate than seen having your girlfriend beside you & having her okay it. Oh boy would I like to have been in your shoes but with my girlfriend. No offense Sal. You understand & [Beulah] wouldn't try cutting in on you.

I guess its Close Situation, next matchlike I'm feeling fine & glad to hear your niece is coming around. Let me hear Bennie & others. Your friend Cong

8 BUSHEL OF MAIL

December 19, 1942

Hello Met,

It's been a long time since I wrote or heard from you. My last letter to you was in November I believe. Well I'm feeling as fine as can be expected. Nothing has hit this boy "yet."

I received a bushel of mail a few weeks ago, cards, packages & letters. I've been trying to answer them as soon as possible but I still have four to answer. Stationery is scarce as hell here, I borrow some from this guy & some from that guy, so I'm getting by until I receive some through the mail.

The heat of 120 degrees isn't bad but these large mosquitoes are a real pain in the neck. They are the largest I've seen & when they bite they draw plenty of blood, then leave a welt the size of a quarter. You kill one & fifty take its place. Aside from that & losing some weight, I'm alright, I guess. Oh, yes, a few heat rashes too.

This letter will probably reach you in the Army someplace but I do hope you get it. I hope you like Army life Met because if you don't it will be that much harder for you. How's the girlfriend Met? Did Julius go yet?

Yesterday I did two weeks laundry of mine & what a job. Generally I wash a few pieces every time I go for a dip but we've been some other place & what water we got was for drinking only. Now we're back in a rest area & have a little time to do things.

Well Metalski we're doing alright for ourselves & it won't be long well have this place lock, stock & barrel. I'll see you in 1943 sometime, I hope. Well so long kid & take care of yourself.

We are using our old APO again.

Your friend,

Butch

PFC. Angelo Buccino 32059032
344th C.A., Btty F APO 502
% Postmaster, San Francisco, Calif.

December 19, 1942

Hello Mel,

It's been a long time since I wrote or heard from you. My last letter to you was in November I believe. Well I'm feeling as fine as can be expected. Nothing has hit this boy yet.

I received a bushel of mail a few weeks ago, cards, packages & letters. I've been trying to answer them as soon as possible but I still have few to answer. Stationery is scarce as hell here, I borrow some from this guy & some from that guy, so I'm getting by until I receive some through the mail.

The heat of 120 degrees isn't bad but these large mosquitoes are a real pain in the neck. They are the largest I've seen & when they bite they draw plenty of blood, then leave a welt the size of a quarter. You kill one & fifty take its place. Aside from that & losing some weight I'm alright, I guess. Oh yes a few heat rashes too.

This letter will probably reach you in the Army someplace but I do hope you get it. I hope you like Army life Mel because if you don't it will be that much harder for you. Hows the girlfriend Mel? Did Julius go yet?

Yesterday I did two weeks laundry of mine & what a job. Usually I wash a few pieces every time I go for a dip but we're in some other place & what water we get was for drinking only. Now we're back in a rest area & have a little time to do things.

Well Matalski was doing alright for awhile & it won't be long will have this place lock, stock & barrel. I'll see you in 1943 sometime, I hope. Well so long kid & take care of yourself. We are using an old A.P.O. again.

Your friend
Tutto

9 OKAY & STILL KICKING

March 21, 1943

Hello Met,

I received your letter of Feb. 23, glad to hear you're doing okay by yourself. Your still in the City You ain't lying you struck it rich. Living in a hotel – eating in a restaurant – maids taking care of your quarters. Well, well, that beats all hell. You lucky stiff. (period.)

I certainly hope you'll be more than a Corporal before your 20 weeks schooling is over. Well don't forget for a John you've done alright. Maybe I'll even have to address your letters Corporal as the next time I hear from you, you may get <??> Could be, you know. Congratulations on our Corporal. That's the stuff kid.

I got a letter from Mike Siluk today & he's still chasing the women around as usual. It was good hearing from him. He was made bread man in Wrights.

Met, many a truth has been spoken in jest. Yes we could meet there someday. Nothing's impossible. But we should meet!

Met there's dam little I can write about from this end. But I'm okay & still kicking that's the main thing.

I saw some native women today. They're nothing to write home about. They just wear skirts & are black as coal. Ugly to boot! Their breasts are very long. I'll take a white girl.

The team won one & lost one today in soft ball. I didn't play as I was too tired after that hike I took.

I'll close now Met & wish you all the best in the world. Give my regards to your brother and girlfriend.

Your Friend,

Ange.

P.Fc Angelo Buccino 32059082
25g C.A. Bty C. A.P.O. 709
% Postmaster, San Fran., Calif
March 21, 1943

Hello Met,

Received your letter of Feb. 23, glad to hear your doing okay by yourself. Your still in the City. You aint saying you struck it rich. Living in a hotel - eating in a restaurant - maids taking care of your quarters. Well, well, that beats all still. Your nucleay stuff! (period)

I certainly hope youll be more than a Pvt. before your 20 weeks schooling is over. You didnt forget I've John - Guiré done alright. Maybe I'd never have to address your letters Corporal as its next time I write you. You may get marked. Could be, you know. Congradulations on your Pvt. now. Thats the stuff kid.

I got a letter from Mike Schulz today & he still chasing the women around as usual. It was good hearing from him. He was made head man in his outfit.

Met, many a truth have been spoken in a jest. Yes we could meet there someday. Nothing's impossible. But we shall meet!

But there dam little I can write about from this end. But I'm okay & still kicking that's the main thing.

I saw some Native women today. They're nothing to write home about. They just wear skirts & are blacker than coal. Ugly to look! Their breast are very long. I'll take a white girl.

The team won one & lost one today in soft ball. I didn't play as I was too stiff after that hike I took.

I'll close now Mil & wish you all the luck in the world. Give my regards to your brother & girlfriend.

Your friend
Ange

10 STIFFIE OWNS A HORSE

April 6, 1943

Hello Met,

Just a few lines to let you know I'm well & still kicking. I've received a few V mail letters from you but I think I've mentioned them before.

A few days ago I received 14 letters & I heard from just about everybody. Stiffie Siluk even wrote. Top that. She said she owns a horse. I got one from Johnny Siluk too.

I'm enclosing a clipping out of the Newark Evening News & hope you recognize him.

I've had a cold for a week & it's really knocking me for a loop.

One of the fellows here gets the Newark Evening News & I get seconds on them. It's good to read about the old home town. I see Belleville is doing okay in basketball. They won 9 out of 10 games and tipped Bloomfield by a large margin. Boy I'll bet Foley pulled his hair out. They had to stop the game for 5 minutes because there was too much noise.

How's tricks with you Met, still attending classes? I am too but it's all old stuff. I'm really surprised that I had forgotten a lot of it too.

Well Metalski, I think it's time to close stations now. I hope this letter finds you okay.

Adios Amigo

Your friend Butch

PS I just received your letter of March 23 which wasn't bad time at all. I bet you ain't lying when you say your writing is difficult to read. V-Mail is hard to read but Met two sheets of V-Mail typewritten can't be beat. That way you have a long letter & it's easy to read.

Well Met somewhere I saw this saying, "Why Worry, when you can pray," I seen that a long time ago. Something I live up to. Your right in saying if you know what war was like you wouldn't make that wish about wanting to join me here. I wouldn't wish this place on a dog or even my worst enemy.

So when you do go, just go over and take your time at bat. Go down slugging if you do go down.

Yesterday I watched a good "Field Day" Boy it was the (mets?). I started to write this a few days ago but forgot to mail it. Today's the eighth. Once before you mentioned a "field day" we had. Well I saw this one but couldn't see the other.

Met remember how Tslinskis's (old man Bra Has) tumblers used to tumble. Likewise!

Last night I thought I'd cough my brains out boy I got it bad. I take pills but they don't seem to do any good.

I got a letter from Andy Bello & he's in the guard house. He went home for 41 days when his kid brother was in that "jam". Can't say I blame him. He was in the Army 18 months & that was an Emergency but they turned him down. Well he furloughed himself home. I'd do that myself if I was in his shoes. He'll be out sometime this month. He got 3 months. Met he blames it all on his brother Nick.

Well Met it is going to be a long time before I meet you and your girlfriend. That's on the level. Well soldier again. I'll close hoping you the best of everything.

Ange

CLIPPING
Lt. William A. Heike Jr. (photo)
Flying Officers Get Commissions
LAKE CHARLES FLYING FIELD, La. – 2nd Lt. William A. Heike, Jr. , 150 Coeyman avenue, Nutley, Army pilot.

P.F.C. Angelo Buccino 32059032
259 C.A. Bty C. A.P.O. 709
% Postmaster, San Fran., Calif
April 6, 1943

Hello Mel,

Just a few lines to let you know I'm well & still kicking. I've received a few V-mail letters from you that's Juanita I have mentioned em before.

A few days ago received 14 letters & heard from just about everybody. Stiffy Siluk even wrote. Say that! She said she runs a horse. I got one from Johnny Siluk too.

I'm enclosing a clipping out of the Newark Evening News & hope you recognize him.

I've had a heavy cold for a week & it's really knocking me for a loop.

One of the fellows here gets the Newark Evening News & I get seconds on it then. It good to read about the old home town. I see Belleville is doing okay in basketball. They won 9 out of 10 games & tipped Bloomfield by a large margin. Boy I'll bet Foley pulled his hair out. They had to stop the game for 5 minutes because there was too much noise.

How tricks with you Mut, still attending classes? I am told that its all old stuff. I'm really surprised that I had forgotten a lot of it too.

Well Mut Calsi, I think its time to close stations now. I hope this letter finds you okay. Adios Amigo

Your friend Butch

P.S. I just received your letter of March 23
which wasn't bad time at all. Met
You aint lying when you say your
writing is difficult to read. V-mail
is hard to read but that two sheets
of V. Mail typewritten can't be beat.
That way you have a long letter & it's
easy to read.

Well Met somewhere I saw this saying
"Why worry, when you can play", seen that
a long time ago. Something I live up to.
Your right in saying if you knew what
war was like you wouldn't make that
wish about wanting to join me here.
I wouldn't wish this place on a dog or even
my worst enemy.

So when you do go, just go over & take
you turn at bat. Go down slugging
if you go down.

Yesterday I watched a good "Field Day"
Boy it was the nuts. I started to write
this a few days ago but forgot to mail
it. Today is the eighth. Once before you

mentioned a "field day" we had. Well I
saw this one but couldn't see the other.
Met remember how Talinskis (Brattos)
trembles used to tremble. Likewise!

Last night I thought I'd cough
my brains out but I got it bad.
Those pills but they don't seem
to do any good.

I got a letter from Andy Butta &
he's in the glass house. He went
home for 41 days when his kid
brother was in that "jam". Can't
say I blame him. He was in the
Army 18 months & that was an emergency
but they turned him down. With my
furlough I'm going home. I'd do that
myself if I were in his shoes. He'll be
out sometime this month. He got 3 months
Met he blows it all in too rather thick.

Well Met it is going to be a long
time before I meet you & your girlfriend
here on the level. Will soldier again
I'll close hoping you the best of everything
Pete

Hal Owen Photo
Lt. William A. Heike Jr.

Flying Officers Get Commissions

Wings for Air Combatant Jerseymen at Fields in the South

Among most recent Jersey flyers to win wings and commissions are:

NAPIER FIELD, Ala.—2d Lt. Lambert R. Lozier, 16 Allen street, Netcong; Army pilot.

RANDOLPH FIELD, Tex.—2d Lt. Louis Staiano of Long Valley; Army pilot.

LAKE CHARLES FLYING FIELD, La.—2d Lt. William A. Heike Jr., 150 Coeyman avenue, Nutley; Army pilot.

GEORGE FIELD, Ill.—2d Lt. Shephard L. Schulz, 294 Roseville avenue, Newark; army pilot.

NAVAL AIR STATION, Jacksonville, Fla.—Ensign William T. Rathbun Jr., 119 Rynda road, South Orange; Navy pilot.

11 MATCHES SCARCE HERE

May 5, 1943

Hello Met,

I just received your letter of April 13th & I'm sure glad to hear from you Pollack. So they're "Indian Givers" eh, give you your rating and if you don't pass they break you. Well Met I don't think that will happen to you as you're going to pass. Or I'll give you a hard boot in the ass when I get you. Do I make myself clear?

Glad to hear your captain of your class soft ball team Out here we haven't played in about two months. Shows are scarce also. The one that used to be near us moved & now you have to go up the line if you want to see it. Well rules state you can go so far from your camp at night. Too many accidents can happen when you travel at night. It may be an enemy & it may be a guard. So I "stood" in bed & the hell with all the shows.

Yes Met what you read about matches being scarce here is true. You're wrong about my not smoking too. I practically eat them. 1 and half packs a day, well when there's excitement its 2 packs or so. I wrote to my girlfriend for a watch and cigarette lighter but later cancelled it because I heard they are hard to get. All you hear is "gimme a light," "let me know when you light up so I can light mine up to" etc. One way & another we manage. The boys who do have lighters are using "white gasoline" as lighter fluid ain't around. They get flint through letters as they're small & universal - so they fit every lighter.

Well I don' know if you have to be a Nation – "Savage as you expressed it" – to live here but I'll never come back here for love or money. The

Nation's helped out a lot Met. Several have received medals for bravery etc. They attend church & seem to contend with life now that the "other half" is gone. They've come down out of the hills & trade with the soldiers. I sent my niece a grass skirt which I got for two packs of cigarettes. They like to be photographed. I took two rolls in one of them villages once. There's nothing beautiful about the women either. Don't worry about this guy Met, I'll get along without it before I have any affairs with them.

You ask how I am receiving the mail, well it's like the weather when it rains it pours. When mail comes in, it comes in by the sack or bushel. You get it usually in lump sums.

Well Met its ten minutes to two & I go on the switch board at two. I'll continue this later. Okay Metalski?

Well I'm back again, boy those two hours flew. Well my daily routine is changed around now. I'm not on the guns, instead in the Ranger Section. It's altogether different.

Say Met did I read right in one of your letters about you guys having maids to clean up? If it's true, man that's rich. Yeah, we don't see a white woman even, let alone clean up for us. Ha ha.

I wrote to Charlie & Tiny not long ago as I got a letter from each of them. Old Charlie is on the ball. He's on a machine gun. (Racket job during peace time) well during war it ain't worth two cents. Life isn't long behind a "typewriter." Gee I think he'd go for mechanics being he knows a lot about motors.

I'll close for now, "Mitchell 2000", hoping this letter finds you in the best of health. Above all Pass that exam. Give my regards to Helen also

Your friend,

Ange

Pfc. Angelo Buccino 32059032
359 C.A. Bty C - A.P.O. 709
% Postmaster, San Fran. Calif.
May 5, 1943

Hello Met,

Just received your letter of April 13th & I'm sure glad to hear from you *Cheeks*. So they're "Indian Gives" eh, giving you your rating & if you don't give they break you. Well Met I don't think that will happen to you as your going to pass. Or I'll give you a *hard look* in the ass when I get you. Do I make myself clear?

Glad to hear your Captain of your Class soft ball team. Out here we haven't played in about two months! Shows are scarce also. The one that used to be near us moved & now you have to go up the line if you want to see it. Well rule states you can't go so far from your camp at night. Too many accidents can happen when you travel at night. It may be an enemy & it may be a guard. So I "stay" in bed & the hell with all the show.

Ya Met what you read about matches being scarce here is true. Your worry about my not smoking too. I gradually cut them. 1½ packs a day, well when they enforced it to 2 packs a so. I wrote to my girlfriend for a watch & cigarette lighter but later cancelled it because I hear they are hard to get. All you hear is "gimme a light"; let me know when you light one up so I can light mine up to "late. One way & another we manage. The boys who do have lighters are using "white gasoline" as lighter fluid ain't around. They get filled through lighters as they're small & unnoticed — or they fix every lighter.

Well I don't know if you chose to be a Marine - *Savage as you expressed it* - to live here but I'll never come back here for love nor money. The Marines helped out a lot Met. Several of received medals for bravery etc. They attend church & seem to be contented with life now that the other half are gone. They come down out of the hills & trade with the soldiers. I sent they there a grass skirt which I got for two packs of cigarettes. They like to be photographed. There are villas in one of these villages now. There is nothing beautiful about the woman either. Don't worry about this guy Mit, i'll get along without it, before I have any affairs with them.

You ask how am I receiving the mail, well its like the weather, when it rains it pours. When mail comes in, it comes in by the cook a bushel. You get it generally in lump sums.

Well Mit its time monotis to tend & I go on the revolted board at two. I'll continue this later. Okay Mitchki!

Well I'm back again, boy those two hours flew. Well my daily routine is changed around now. I'm not on the line, instead in the _____ station. Its altogether different.

Say Mit, did I read right in one of your letters about you guys having maids to clean up? If it's true, man that's rich. Yeah we dont see a white woman even, let alone clean up for us. ha ha.

I wrote to Charlie & Tiny not long ago as I got a letter from each of them. Old Charlie is on the ball. He's on a machine gun. (Rackety job during peace time) well during war it ain't worth ten cents. Life ain't long behind a typewriter. He thinks he'd go in for mechanics being he knows a lot about motors.

I'll close now, "Mitchell 2000", hoping this letter finds you in the best of health. Give all Pa's that exam. Give my regards & all racks. Your friend
Nunzi

12 RUTH ROBERTSON WROTE

May 15, 1943

Hello Met,

Just received your letter of April 24th & I was glad to hear from you Pal. Yes we had another Field Day the other day but that's everyday stuff here.

Yeah Met I guess your girlfriend is right. The minute you boast of something, it goes sour. I do wish you luck in getting a transfer nearer to home so you can get married. Hope the Fortune Teller is right in her predictions.

Oh my cold is gone now & it was the worst one I ever had. Where the hell did you get the idea there were WACs here? But you ain't lying when you say I'd like to have one in a fox hole with me. So you guys had to move into another hotel eh?

Yes I'm getting my share of mail these days. Man I really like to hear from people.

Oh yes, Miss Robertson told me to tell you, you weren't pulling the wool over the teacher's eyes. Margaret Frost has a baby boy 2 years old. My kid brother wrote to her also. If you want to drop her a line her address is Ruth Robertson 1 Essex Street Belleville N.J.

Say Met I saw a show the other night & the picture was "Pride of the Yankees" & it was very good. I've tried to see that picture for a long time. Well we'll be seeing shows again as the show is nearby again.

Arnold Thiting is on this island too but I've been here a helluva a long time & I haven't bumped in to him yet. Miss Robertson told me he was here.

I am sitting beside the radio man & I showed him your letter. He took a two months course & can now send out 19 words per minute. He said you're going good & should hit 30 words by the end of your class.

Well Met I'm feeling fine & hope to hear the same from you. Let me know how that transfer works out. Give my regards to your brothers & Helen.

Your friend
Ange

PS I just got a letter from Phill – he weighs 250 pounds. Can you imagine. He has two kids too.

Miss Robertson letter
Written April 23 & 24th
Dear Angelo,

Your letters arrived on consecutive days. I was most disappointed when I thought the censor was keeping your pictures as well as a paragraph, but the second letter made me think better of him. I know they will be much appreciated by others at school tomorrow.

Is food, lack of exercise, or much exercise and much food which has given you the extra pounds? Looks as if the govt would have to let out a few seams and buttons on your uniform.

No one has told me exactly where you are, but my knowledge of the geography in that part of the world has improved greatly in the past year or so, due to my natural curiosity – also my favorite crossword puzzle in the N.Y. Times *makes me go over that area with a microscope, so I am guessing – maybe incorrectly.*

Arnold Thiting is resting and fighting malaria on Guadalcanal – and true Marine hoping for Round II.

Salvatore Pedalino has had 3 months in a Navy uniform, but hasn't yet been fired with the enthusiasm of the other fellows. Gus Vaccaro [Coxswain Gus F. Vaccaro, 20, was killed in action Feb. 26, 1945] *also in blues is loving a gunner's training and itching to be at sea.*

Tell Mitchell M. that we teachers could usually read the stuff our people wrote, even tho' we may pretend we can't. Maybe that is where I got my love for puzzles.

Carmen Petti was in – on furlough from Carolina in photography training for the air corps. Your kid brother wrote a very nice letter, too, with no particular news for you I guess. He told me he loved mail "no matter who it's from." I know he didn't mean it the way it sounded, but we all got a laugh just the same.

Margaret Frost is married and has a nice little boy – 2 or 3 yrs. old. Marie Frost takes more care of him than his mother but I guess he knows to whom he belongs when he gets into things as all boys do.

Miss Nelson gets to see us during rationing days. The H.S. teachers are sent out to the grade schools so we get a chance to catch up on news of old friends.

Don't let the idea of the boys from England and Africa getting furlough bother you too much. The only ones I know of who are back came for medical treatment. The others are still needed over there to finish a job we've begun. Bernard Ingo was in the hospital in Africa for shrapnel wounds a time back. A sailor friend he made on his way over on the troop ship brought back the story on one of his layovers in N.Y.

Our usual vacation at Easter is omitted since we had time out in Feb. to conserve fuel. But I fooled them. I took the week to spend in bed to get rid of the cold I have had all winter. Right now I've had enough of staying "put" and am ready to go to school a new person tomorrow. I guess I shan't start my evening job until about Wed.

On Tuesday we have a shower for Phyl Calicchio who is to be married to her attorney next Sunday.

I think I've told you everything I know.

Keep smiling. Your teeth shine as they always did!! You see I remember yours, Tony Schiagvo's Carmen Macaluso's and a few others.

Sincerely
Ruth Robertson

Pfc Angelo Buccino 32059032
259 C.A. Bty C. A.P.O. 709
c/o Postmaster, San Fran. Calif.
May 15, 1943

Hello Met,

Just received your letter of April 24th & was glad
to hear from you Pal. Yes we had another Field
Day the other day but that's everyday stuff here.
Yeah Met I guess your girlfriend is right. The
minute you boast of something it goes sour.
I do wish you luck in getting a transfer nearer
to home so you can get married. Hope the
fortune teller is right in her predictions.

Oh my cold is gone now & it was the
worst one I ever had. Where the hell did
you get the idea there were fleas here. But you
aint lying when you say I'd like to live on
in a fox hole with one. So you guys had to
move into another hotel eh.

Yes I'm getting my share of the mail these
days. Man I really like to hear from people.
Oh yes Miss Robertson told me to tell
you, you weren't pulling the wool over
the teacher's eyes. Margaret just had a
baby boy 2 years old. My kid brother
wrote to her also. If you want to drop
her a line her address is Miss Ruth Robertson
1 Easy St.
Bellvith, N.J.

Say Mit I saw a show the other night & the picture was "Pride Of The Yankees" & it was very good. I've tried to see that picture for a long time. Will will be seeing shows again as the show is near by again.

Arnold Stuting is on this Island too but I've been here a hell a long time & haven't bumped into him yet. Miss Robertson told me he was here. I'll try to locate him.

I am sitting beside the radio now & school him for later. He took a two minute cause & can now send out 19 words per minute. He said I'm going good & should hit 30 words by the end of my class.

Well Mit I'm feeling fine & hope the same from you. Let me know how that transfer works out. Give my regards to your brother & John.

Your friend
Inge.

P.S. Just got a letter from Bill — he weighs 250 pounds. Can you imagine. He has two kids too.

1 E. ssex Street
Belleville, N.J.
Easter Sunday.
(Apr. 25, 1944)

Dear Angelo,

Your letters arrived on consecutive days. I was most disappointed when I thought the censor was keeping your pictures as well as a paragraph, but the second letter made me think better of him. I know they will be much appreciated by the others at school tomorrow.

Is food, lack of exercise, or much exercise and much food which has given you the extra pounds? Spoke as if the gov't would have to let out a few seams and buttons on your uniform.

No one has told me exactly where you are, but my knowledge of the geography of that part of the world has improved greatly in the past year or so, due to my natural curiosity — also my favorite crossword puzzle in the N.Y. times strikes me so over that edge, with a mistake or two, so I am guessing — maybe incorrectly ....

Arnold Thiting is resting and fighting malaria on Guadalcanal and true Marine hoping for Round II.

Silvatore Pikalino has had 3 months in a navy uniform, but hasn't yet been fired with the enthusiasm of the other fellows. Jim Vaccaro also in blues is loving a gunner's training and itching to be at sea.

Tell Mitchell M. that we teachers can usually read the stuff our pupils write, even tho' we may pretend we can't. Maybe that is where I got my cape for puzzles.

Carmen Petti was in — on furlough from Carolina in photography training of the air corps. Your kid brother wrote a very nice letter, too, with no particular news for you I guess. He told me he loved mail "no matter

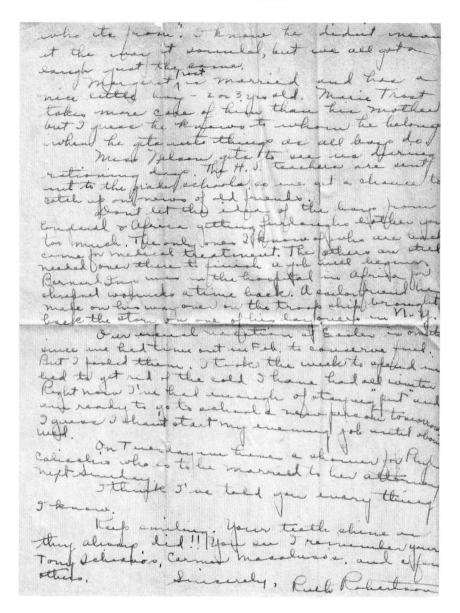

who its from". I know he didn't mean
it the way it sounded, but we all got a
laugh just the same.

Margaret Trost is married and has a
nice little boy - 2 or 3 yrs old. Marie Trost
takes more care of him than his mother
but I guess he knows to whom he belongs
when he gets hurt things as all boys do.

Miss Nelson gets to see us during
rationing days. The H.S. teachers are sent
out to the grade schools so we get a chance to
catch up on news of old friends.

Don't let this idea of the boys from
England & Africa getting furloughs bother you
too much. The only ones I know of who are here
came for medical treatment. The others are still
needed over there to finish a job well begun.
Bernard Trost was in the hospital in Africa for
shrapnel wounds a time back. A sailor friend he
made on his way over on the troop ship brought
back the story on one of his layovers in N.Y.

Our school reception at Emsley is on still
since we had time out in Feb. to conserve fuel.
But I fooled them. It took the week to spend in
bed to get rid of the cold I have had all winter.
Right now I've had enough of staying "put" and
am ready to go to school & new pep on tomorrow.
I guess I shan't start my evening job until
well.

On Tuesday we have a shower for Phyl
Calicchio who is to be married to her attorney
next Sunday.

I think I've told you everything
I know.

Keep smiling. Your teeth shine as
they always did!! You see I remember your
Tony Schiario, Carmen Massaluso, and other
others.

Sincerely, Ruth Robertson

13 I REMEMBER JOYCE MORE

June 3, 1943

Hello Met,

I received two letters of yours yesterday – May 7 & 16th, Pretty good if you ask me. Say Met did you ever the story of the "Gold & Silver Shield"? Well it seems that two knights approached a mounted shield from opposite sides. One knight said – my what a gold shield, the other said: It's a Silver Shield, well one word lead to another & they had a duel. One was killed. The victor looks up & sees that the shield was gold on one side & silver on the other. So they had been both right. I forget what the lesson of that story was.

That brings us to that debate of ours Met, we could both argue from now to doomsday & we'd both be right, so let's park it.

It was news to me about Val visiting the Woodbridges, etc. Small world ain't it. Yeah I remember the old man Pal. I remember Joyce more though. Remember the dance she put on down in camp near the pond. She sure wiggled around plenty. Not saying what we used to do to her. All in all I don't think anybody got into the "ball park", a lot of guys got on bases and struck out though. Ha ha.

So you asked your ole man to move the pigeon coop if he heard a bomb coming, eh? Some joke I'll say. Met [CONTENT CUT OUT] big ass into the nearest hole & shit with thinking about personal belongings etc. My hide is what interests me most. I ain't shittin you either.

I'm glad about Joe being able to get out too Met but I burn up knowing no defense plant will take him because he isn't a citizen. He has his half papers etc. but the best he could do was get his old job back. He's married & can't afford to be choosy. Yeah kid when you're married you have to put your pride in your back pocket & just take it. Now when you're single & don't like your job you just leave, & rely on your Mother. Joe is no slouch when it comes to working Met. I know. I only wish he could land a decent job somewhere.

Glad to hear your coming along okay in radio school. Passed 26 words per minute eh & eight weeks to go. Well I think you ought to fit thru the 30 mark before school is over.

For the past few months I've been losing weight right along but as long as I feel good & stay in one piece, I've got no kicks coming.

Met I put in for O.C.S. & in the near future I go before the Board. That is if things go along accordingly. I've attended trig classes for the past month & that helps a lot in the long run. I look upon this golden opportunity & I'm hoping for the best.

Well Met ol boy I'll so say so long until next time. Hope this letter finds you well. Give Helen my regards & don't forget.

So long Pal

Your friend

Ange

P.F.C. Angelo Buccino 32059032
254 C.A. Bty C. A.P.O. 709
℅ Postmaster, San Fran. Calif.
~~2nd~~ June 3, 1943

Hello Mat,

I received two letters of yours yesterday - May 7 & 16th. Pretty good if you ask me. Say Mat did you ever hear the ~~story~~ of the "Gold & Silver Shield"? Well it seems that two knights approached a mounted shield from opposite sides. One knight said - my what a gold shield! the other said: its a silver shield, well one word led to another & they had a duel. One was killed. The victor looked up & saw that the shield was gold on one side & silver on ~~the~~ other. So they had been both right. I forget what the lesson of that story was.

That brings us to that debate of ours Mat, we could both argue from now to doomsday & we'd both be right, so lets park it.

It was new to me about Val inviting the midshipmen etc. I small world ain't it. Yeah I remember the ole man Val. I remember Joyce more though. Remember the dance she put on down in camp near the pond. She sure wiggled around plenty. Not saying what we used to do to her. All in all I think anybody got into the "ball park", a lot of guys got on base & struck out though. ha ha.

So you asked your ole man to move the onion corp[?] or he heard a bird coming eh. Sounds like 3d say. Mat _____ big ass into ~~the~~ nearest hole & shit with bumping about ~~personal~~ belongings etc. My hide is what interests me most. I ain't shittin you either.

I'm glad about Joe being able to get out too Mat but I burn up knowing an defense plant will take him because he ain't a citizen. He has his first papers etc but that but he could do was get his old job back. He's married & can't afford to be choosey. Yeah kid when your married you have to put your pride in your back pocket & just take it. Now when you single & don't like your job you just leave, & rely on your Mother. Joe is no slouch when it comes to working Mat. However, I only wish he could land a decent job somewhere.

Glad to hear you coming along okay in radio school. Passed 26 words per minute eh & eight weeks to go. Well I think you ought to hit the 30 mark before school is over.

For the past few months I've been loosing weight right along but as long as I feel good & stay in one piece, I've got no kicks coming.

Mat I put in for O.C.S. & in the near future I go before the Board. That is if things go along accordingly. I've attended the classes for the past month & that helps a lot in the long run. I look upon this as my golden opportunity & I'm hoping for the best.

Well Mat ol boy I'll say so long until next time. Hope this letter finds you well. Give Helen my regards & don't forget.

So long Pal

Your friend
George

14 TINY FILLED OUT

July 3, 1943

Hello Met,

I received two letters of yours dated June 14 & 19th. That's something. The mail is sure coming in pretty regular these days.

So somebody told Miss Robertson about you eh. Well it's a good thing it's all good or you'd have plenty of explaining to do.

I got a letter from Tiny and there was four pictures in it. Yes I was surprised to see how he filled out too. I have that on him in the trunks too. He looks like he can lick the whole family now.

I never saw that Wave that was supposed to be here so I wouldn't know what she looks like. Your right in saying what you did though. Just as long as it was a white woman, she'd be an Angel.

You ain't kidding about the Field Days Pal. Its every day stuff now. Pat was wounded but he's okay now. He'd better be! He's my "best man".

Thanks for getting me the lighter Met. Boy I can sure use one. I'll let you know when I receive it.

By the time this reaches you your classes will be over. Let me know your new address as soon as possible.

Say Met your wrong in saying shoot anything that doesn't speak English. Hell haven't you heard that some of them were educated in the States & can talk better than you or I. There's other tell-tale signs though. Some habits – just like the rats I used to trap.

You ask what is the first thing I'm going to do when I get back. Well I had tried to get married but Marie don't see things that way. She's waited this long she may as well wait till it's over.

But if you meant coming back after the war – yea it would be marriage. I hope I'm not stuck out here till it ends because the end ain't near! If this mess is over by 1944, the drinks are on me.

Its true we're getting into high gear met but there's a lot of places to be taken that will take time. You can disagree with me as that's only my opinion. We shall see ole timer.

I'm feeling the best ever Met – no kidding. I hope I stay that way too. I saw a few good pictures this week. Andy Hardy's Double Life & they All Kissed the Bride. You ought to hear the guys yell when she (the bride) said: "If I want a sneak I'll hire a Jap."

By the way Met (going back to your love affair for a minute) what makes you say enough time has been lost already. Your wrong soldier. There's plenty of time, you or her isn't 30 years old you know.

Adios Amigo

Butch

PS Here's a few jokes Met

A girl asks her boyfriend if he wants to see the hair on her chest in which he agrees. She lifts up her dress about hip length and her boyfriend exclaims: "That isn't your chest!" "Oh Yes: says the girl. "Before my marriage it was my tool chest now that I'm divorced it's my community chest.

[BOTTOM OF LETTER PAGE CUT BY CENSOR]

T/5. Angelo Buccino 32059032
259 C.A. Bty. C - A.P.O. 709
% P/M - San Fran. Calif.
July 3, 1943

Hello Mut,

Received two letters of yours dated
June 14 & 19th. Thats something. The mail
is sure coming in pretty regular these
days.

So somebody else told Miss Robertson
about you eh. Well its a good thing its all
good or youd have plenty of explaining to
do.

Got a letter from Tiny & there was four
pictures in it. Jo) was surprised to see
how he filled out too. Than that one
of him in the trunks too. He looks like
he can lick the whole family now.
I never saw that Mary that was
supposed to be here so I wouldnt know
what she looks like. Your right in

saying what you did though. Just as long it were a white woman, she'll be an Angel.

You ain't kidding about the Field Days Pal. Its every day stuff now. Pat was wounded but he's okay now. He'd better be. He's my "Rat man".

Thanks for getting me the lighter Met. Boy I can sure use one. I'll let you know when I receive it.

By the time this reaches you your classes will be over. Let me know your new address as soon as possible.

Say Met your wrong in saying shoot anything that don't speak English. Hell haven't you heard that some of them were educated in the States & can talk better than you or I. There's other tell tale signs though. Small habits first like the rats I used to trap.

You ask what is the first thing Im goyny to do when I get back. Well I had hoped to get married but Marie don't see things that way. She's waited this long she may as well wait till its over. But if you meant I coming back after the war - yes it would be marriage. Thogo Im not stuck out here till it ends because the end aint new! If this Mess is over in 1944, the drinks are on me.

Its true were getting into high gear Mpt but theres a lot of places to be taken that will take time. You can disagree with me as thats only my opinion. We shall see ob time.

Im feeling the best ever Mpt - no kidding. Thoge I stay that way too. I saw a few good pictures this week. Andy Hardys Double Life + They All Kissed the Bride. You ought to hear the guys yell when she said: If I want a drink Ill hire a Sap -

By the way Met (going back to your love affair for a minute) what makes you say enough time has been lost already? You wrong soldier. There plenty of time, you or her isn't 30 years old you know.

Adios Amigo

P.S. Heres a few jokes Met.

Butch

A girl asks her boyfriend if he wants to see the hair on her Chest in which he agrees. She lifts her dress about hip length and her boyfriend exclaims: "That isn't your chest". "Oh Yes" says the girl. "Before my marriage it was my hope chest, after my marriage it was my tool chest, now that I'm divorced it's my community chest.

In Memorandum

At the close of existence when we've climbed life's golden stair
And the chilly winds of autumn toss our silvery hair
When we feel our manhood ebbing & mine up to life's last ditch
When we find the faithful Peter, sleeping soundly at the switch.
But all mighty ain't it awful? for it makes a fellow sick
When the painful fact confronts us, that we ne'er got a fellow chick
That he never will bristle on wet & misty day
When some maiden shows her stocking, in that naughty - funny way.
Oh my poor loyal king pin, how my heart goes out to you
For I cannot remember all the stunts you used to do.
How you charmed the maidens & the matrons, & the ducking widows too
How you had the whole bunch begging for just a little piece of you
Think you now that I'll forget you, just because you seem so dead
And because when I command you, you cannot lift your droopy head
No indeed valiant comrade, naught shall rob you of your fame
Henceforth you shall be my pleasure & I'll love you just the same.

An Eye Full

A Tramp leaned against the wall
Beside a window frame
Inside he heard some voices
He heard the girl exclaim
"You cannot do it that way"
But you see I cannot wait
You always let it waffle
Dear, cant you keep it straight
If you cannot do it that way
You cannot do it at all
I think that yours is much to big
And mine is much too small
Lets try it this way now
And be careful of my dress
If you let it slip out now
You'll make an awfull mess
Please have a little patience
And you'll surely win
So now you've got it started
for god sakes push it in

The Tramp got so excited
Through the window gave he drew
To see a man & woman
Putting a stove pipe in the stove. //

15 JERSEY MET OR CALIFORNIA

August 2, 1943

Hello Met,

Received two letters of yours dated June 28 and July 19th. Sorry to hear you bought the cigarette lighter for me and couldn't send it. I can't help with the mail rules as they change faster than the weather. At the time I asked you for it all that was needed – it be censored. I don't know what it is now Met. But present this letter to the Postal Clerk. I need a cigarette lighter out here & I'm sure it's okay.

Met I just went and asked my Lieutenant about it & he said just show this letter of request for the lighter to the clerk. I thought it'd be that way but I just wanted to make sure. Don't forget envelope and letter. That's that!

I'll say you never got to first base, I'll even go further than that – you never got into the ball park. Ha ha. Yes Yes times have changed. Good causes too. Wish you all the luck in the world Pal.

Met I'm sorry I mentioned my trying out for O.C.S. to my friends as they all wished me luck. Well as luck would have it I never went up before the Board. I'm pretty far from that Board & Saturday I heard I was supposed to appear Friday. So you can see where I stand. You can't give me that boot in the tail Met yet anyway. If anything comes of it I'll let you know.

Ah, so you're out in Sunny California! Sunny my eye, as George Raft said, we only have 2 foot of dew there. (Picture: Stage Door Canteen)

Boy you sound as though you really need that rugged training. Pal you take my advice and don't miss a minute of it. And I ain't lying!

Met if you do go over, I too wish we could run across each other. Got a letter from Joe (Chris) Giron & he's been out this way. Seen plenty too. Action of course. Here's his address Joseph J. Giron Jr. USS Brooklyn – c/o PM NY NY (correction last page) He'll keel overboard with surprise.

I see you're a rolling stone. Well Pal you won't gather any moss anyway. I hope I can make that cross country trip some day.

Boy that Miss Robertson is a "shrewd particle" with her jig saw puzzles. She mentioned hearing from you & that's was at the bottom of it. Yes. Yes.

Met as you can see I'm still at large. Hope that's one number I don't draw. No how! I was sick in bed for a week but I'm okay now. God Bless them Pills.

I don't see any shows anymore as their ain't any in our area. Boy I miss them plenty. I did make the best of it while it lasted though – now I'll just have to make up my mind I must get along without it. That ain't hard. Eh, Met?

Met one of these days you'll get a little token from me. I won't tell you as I want it to be a surprise – to the both of you. You'd never guess in a million tries. So don't rack your brain.

In case your overseas would you want me to still send it to you, Helen or your home? I'll try to get it off within two weeks. But this is just in case I can't. So Met answer as soon as possible.

I don't think of that "day" Met as it's a long way off. Just wait & see. Well there's nothing like wishing.

I'm feeling fine & hope this letter finds you well & in the best of health. Your friend Ange

P.S. (Robertson received a letter in 6 days from me.)

PS #2 I wonder if I should call you Jersey Met or California. Why? Well you wish you were back in Jersey but you're in California. I'll toss a coin. You win California!

Adios Amigo

If you had wished for California you would have probably ended up in Jersey. Could be?

Pvt. A. Buccino 3205 9032
259 C.A. Bty. D. - A.P.O. 709
℅ P.M. San Fran. Calif.

August 2, 1943

Hello Mel,

Received two letters of yours dated June 28 & July 19th. Sorry to hear you bought the cigarette lighter for me & couldn't send it. I can't keep up with the mail rules as they change faster than the weather. At the time I asked you for it all that was needed - it be censored. I don't know what it is now Mel. But present this letter to the Postal Clerk. I need a cigarette lighter out here & I'm sure its okay.

Mel I just went and asked my Lieutenant about it & he said just show this letter of request for the lighter to the Clerk. I thought it'd be that way but I just wanted to make sure. Don't forget envelope & letter. That's that!

I'll say you never got to first base, I'll even go further than that. You never got into the ball park. ha ha. Yo Yo times have changed. Ford cause too. (Helen) Wish you all the luck in the world Pal.

Met I'm sorry I mentioned my trying out for O.C.S. To my friends as they all wished me luck. Well as luck would have it I never went up before the Board. I'm pretty fur from that Board & Saturday I heard I was supposed to appear Friday. So you can see where I stand. You can't give me that boot in the tail just yet anyway. If anything comes of it I'll let you know.

Ah, so Your out in Sunny California! Sunny my eye, as George Raft said, we only have 2 foot of dew there. (Stage Door Canteen) (a picture)

Boy you sound as though you really need that rugged training. Pal you take my advice + don't miss a minute of it. And I aint lying.

But if you do go over, I too wish we could run across each other. Got a letter from Joe (Chris) Siron + he's been out this way. Sun plenty too. Section of cause. Here's his address: Joseph J. Siron Jr. — U.S.S. Brooklyn — c/o P.M. N.Y. N.Y. Hill

feel overboard with surprise.   Correction last page

I see Jim a rolling stone, well Pal you won't gather any moss anyway. Hope Jean make that Cross Country trip some day.

Boy that Miss Robertson is a "shrewd particle" with her jig saw puzzles. She mentioned hearing from you + that's was at the bottom of it. Yo. Yo.

But as you can see I'm still at large. Hope thats in number I don't draw. No how! I was sick in bed for a week but I'm okay now. God Bless them Pills.

I can't see any shows anymore as there aren't any in our area. Boy miss them plenty. I did make the best of it while it lasted though - now I'll just have to make up my mind I must get along without it. That ain't hard. Eh, Mel?

One of these days you'll get a little token from me. I won't tell you as I want it to be a surprise - to the both of you. You'd never guess in a million trys. So don't rack your brain.

In case your overseas would you want me to still send it to you, Helen or your home? I'll try to get it off within two weeks. But this is just in case I can't. So Mel answer as soon as possible.

I don't think of that "day" Mel as it's a long way off. Just wait & see. Well there's nothing like wishing.

I'm feeling fine & hope this letter finds you well & in the best of health. Your friend

PS. (Robertson received a letter in 6 days from me.) Lange

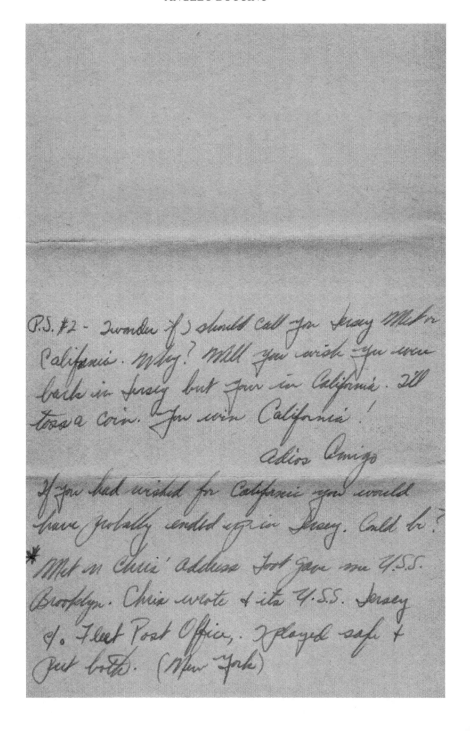

P.S. #2 - I wonder if I should call you Jersey Metro California. Why? Will you wish you were back in Jersey but you're in California. I'll toss a coin. You win California!

Adios Amigo

If you had wished for California you would have probably ended up in Jersey. Could be?

* Met in Chici' Address Toot gave me U.S.S. Brooklyn. Chicie wrote & its U.S.S. Jersey c/o Fleet Post Office, I played safe & put both. (New York)

16 FLINT & FLUID

Sept. 13, 1943

Hello California,

I received your letter of August 26th and it was good hearing from you again. I really hit the jackpot this week – in mail I mean. I also got your package. Thanks a lot Met. You don' have to send me Flint & fluid as the boys here have plenty of flint & we use a few drops of white gas & it's just as good & more abundant.

You're right about Val not liking his outfit. If he'd a kept it to himself he'd still be a Corporal. I should talk, eh Pollack!

Met that training you're getting you'll never regret. I can't tell you what kind of terrain you'll be fighting in but you've seen pictures & should have a fair idea. I can't ask you about your guns Met but I see your getting variety. That's the best way of learning

Well Fella I sure wish you luck in getting your furlough. I might add that if I were in your shoes & anxious to get married Pal I wouldn't wait for a furlough, I'd make my own. But stick it out till your settled. That isn't far off. I may sound nuts to you fella, but I'm not. I'm giving you a piece of advice. Whether it's good or bad depends on how you look at it.

Maybe your mother will get her wish at that. This world's full of surprises. Or should I say disappointments?

Met, those drinks you mentioned will have to wait a year, maybe more. There's no outlook in my getting home for quite some time. It's been a long time Mitchell since I last saw my folks and girlfriend. But I'm still hanging on. A break may come through all of those dark clouds yet.

Going back to that bit of advice a minute. Out here we say "If I knew then, what I know now." I for one can kick myself in the ass for not getting married first. Things happened to fast & before I woke up I was somewhere in the Pacific. Well, now I'll just have to grin and bear it. I seen a white woman last week for the first time in one year. She was a Nurse and worked on the Air Transports. It was short lived but nice to know those creatures are still in existence.

Met I got a boot in the tail coming as I went up for O.C.S. but didn't pass. I'm thinking of trying again in a few months. Your one up on me Pal & I'll pay off. Ha Ha.

I seen some good pictures lately such as Random Harvest, Yankee Doodle Dandy – Mrs. Miniver & also a few others.

Well I won't see any for a few weeks as the projector went to another Battery for a week or so. We alternate.

I lost my shirt this month in Crap. The dice changed faster than the wind. I'm due Met as I've lost steady the past four months. (Four pays, I should say.) That's eight months to you.

Well Pollack I guess I'll sign off till next time. Give my regards to the boys & let me have Donkeys address as soon as possible.

I received your package & now I'm waiting to hear you received mine. Then everything will be all right!

So long Pollack

Regards to Helen

Ange.

Pvt. Angelo Buccino 32059032
254 C.A. Bty. B. A.P.O. 709
% P.M. San Fran. Calif.
Sept. 13th - 1943

Hello California,

Received your letter of August 26th
& it was good hearing from you again.
Really hit the jackpot this past
week - in mail I mean. Also got your
package. Thanks a lot Mel. You don't
have to send me flint & fluid as
the boys here have plenty of flint &
we use a few drops of white gas & it's
just as good & more abundant.

You right about Val not liking
his outfit. If he'd a kept it to himself
he'd still be a Corporal. I should talk
eh Pollack!

Met that training your getting
you'll never regret. I can't tell you
what kind of terrain you'll be fighting
in but I've seen pictures & I should

have a fair idea. I can't ask you
about your guns but but I see your
getting variety. That's the best way of
learning.

Well fella I sure wish you luck
in getting your furlough. I might add
that if I were in your shoes & anxious
to get married, that I wouldn't wait for
a furlough, I'd make my own. But
stick it out till your settled. That isn't
far off. I may sound nuts to you fella
but I'm not. I'm giving you a piece of
advice. Whether its good or bad depends on
how you look at it.

Maybe your Mother will get her
wish at that. This world's full of
surprises. Or should I say disappointments.

Well those drinks you mentioned
will have to wait a year, maybe
more. There's no outlook in my getting
home for quite sometime. It's been a
long time Mitchell since I last saw

my folks & girlfriend. But I'm still hanging on. A break may come through those dark clouds yet.

Going back to that bit of advice a minute. Out here we say "If I knew then, what I know now." For one can kick myself in the ass for not getting married first. Things happened to fast & before I woke up I was somewhere in the Pacific. Well now I just have to grin & bear it.

I seen a white woman last week for the first time in one year. She was a Nurse & worked on the Air Transports. It was short lived but nice to know those creatures are still in existence.

Well I got a boot in the tail coming as I went up for O.C.S. but didn't pass. I'm thinking of trying again in a few months. Keep the eye on me Pal & I'll pay off. Ha Ha.

Iv seen some good pictures lately such as :- Random Harvest, the Yankee Doodle Dandy - Miss Minerva & also a few others.

Well I won't see any for a few weeks as the projector went to another Battery for a week or so. We alternate.

Lost my shirt this month in Africa. The air changed faster than the wind. I'm due West as I've lost steadily the past four months. (Four gays, I should say.) Thats eight months to you.

Well Pollack I guess I'll sign off till next time. Give my regards to the boys & let me have Yonkers address as soon as possible.

Received your package & now I'm waiting to hear you received mine. Then everything will be allright!

So long Pollack -
Regards to Helen.
Ange

80

Here one for your Met,

A school teacher told the children
to bring different articles to school
to represent different songs.

So she told three of the boys to
stand up before the class room & give
out.

1st boy had a flash light, so the
teacher asked him what that represented.
he said:- When the lights go on, all over the world.

The 2nd boy had a broken flare & a
song that represented. He said:- Coming
In On A Wing & a Prayer.

The 3rd little boy stood there & let
his pants fall down. The teacher asked
him what in the world that represented
He said:- For Me & My Gal.

17 HELLO, CALIFORNIA

May 21, 1945

Hello Helen,

Just a note to let you know I received your letter the other day. I was glad to hear from you & I was wondering why no answer. But your forgiven as I'm beginning to see the light (as the song goes.)

I'm busy driving a truck around Camp & last week I went on a Convoy that took me away from camp for two days. Boy the bed sure fits good after that trip.

I've done quite a bit of skating at the rink they have here. I go about 3 or 4 nights a week. Did you ever roller skate? Haven't taken in the sights around town yet but eventually I'll get around to it.

No doubt you've heard of the Point System, etc. Well I just barely cleared the fence with 88 points. I don't know when I'll get out but just knowing I'm slated makes me drool. How I'd love to get back to my wife and be a civilian again. Well I can dream can't I? I was thinking of having her out here with me but I priced the rooms & its highway robbery $40 for 1 room – $60 for two if you can find an opening. Well that will never do for me.

I'll wait another month and put in for a furlough. The reason I'm waiting is to see how large the next quota will be as I wish my next trip East is permanent. Period! So why throw $100 into the winds.

I'm glad you like the set up there – it makes things easier for you. Now if Met was a sailor – his ship may put into port every so often but since he's not – well – Your guess is as good as mine. Liking where you're staying helps a great deal too.

Well how long it will last now who can say? I hope its short & sweet So we all can go home & back to our normal ways of living.

Glad to hear Met made you a bracelet Helen out there you can't buy gifts etc. So you try a hand at making something in your spare time. If & when Met does send you more gifts you'll find what I said is true.

Between you and I Helen – I like California better than Jersey. This place is a paradise. Down here the weather is fine – plenty of jobs. Well it's having your relatives back East etc. that makes you want to go back. My parents are old and nearly helpless as far as speech & legal matters are concerned & somebody's got to take care of them. But California is nice.

Helen I'll make that trip after pay day as I'll feel safe to travel. I have another wife to see in Alameda also. She's staying there & waiting for her sailor husband to return. She's my wife's best girlfriend. I'll write & let you know & I'll keep your telephone number handy too.

Are there nights you go out? I don't want to miss you when I come up. It will probably be over a week end most likely. Sat. night or Sunday. I'll let you know ahead of time for sure.

I just hope I can live up to the build up Met gave me. Ha ha. In case Bruno didn't tell you when we were up to their place we saw your room – wedding pictures etc. You were adorable Helen & Met was handsome. I know you have a fine man for a hubby & vice versa. Someday you'll drop in on us & we'll show you our pictures etc. too. Okay.

Say if you want to send Met something the 1st thing I'd say he'd like is pictures of you. If you can – get some film & send it to him as somebody may have camera in his outfit. Write first & ask if he'd like some film & to state the size. Pictures will live on & on. Don't you forget that.

Well Helen I'll close for now- hoping to see you in the near future.

Your friend, Ange

May 21, 1945

Hello Helen,

Just a few lines to let you know I received your letter the other day. I was glad to hear from you & I was wondering why no answer. But you forgive as I'm beginning to see the light. (as the song goes.)

I'm busy driving a truck around Camp & last week I went on a Convoy that took me away from camp for two days. Boy the bed sure felt good after that trip.

I've done quite a bit of skating at the rink thing have here. I go about 3 or 4 nights a week. Did you ever roller skate? Haven't taken in the sights around town yet but eventually I'll get around to it.

No doubt you've heard of this point system etc. Well I just barely cleared the fence with 88 points. I don't know when I'll get out but just knowing normal ways of living.

Glad to hear that made you a bracelet Helen out there. You cant buy gifts etc so you try a hand at making something in your space time. If & when that does send you more gifts youll find what I said is true.

Between you & I Helen — I like California better than Jersey. This place is a paradise. Down here the weather is fine — plenty of jobs. Well its having your relatives back East etc that makes you want to go back. My parents are old & nearly helpless as far as speech & legal matters are concerned & somebody got to take care of them. But California is nice.

Helen I'll make that trip after pay day as I'll feel safe to travel. I have another wife to see in Alameda also. She's staying there & waiting for her sailor husband to return. She's my wife's best girlfriend. I'll write & let you know & I'll keep your telephone number handy too. Are there nights you go out? I don't

I'm slated make me drool. How I'd love to get back to my wife & be a civilian again. Well I can dream can't I? I was thinking of having her out here with me but figured the rooms & its highway robbery $40 for 1 room — $60 for two. if you can find an opening. Well that will mean do you see.

I'll wait another month & put in for a furlough. The reason I'm waiting is to see how large this next quota will be as I wish my next trip east is permanent. Period! So why throw $100 into the winds.

I'm glad you like the set up there — it makes things easier for you. Now if Mut was a sailor — his ship may put into port every so often but since he's not — well ———! Your guess is as good as mine. Taking when your staying helps a great deal too!

Well how long it will last now — who can say? I hope its short & sweet so we all can go home & back to our

want to miss you when I come up.
It will probably be over a week end
most likely. Sat. night or Sunday. I'll
let you know ahead of time for sure.

Hope Jean live up to the build up
Met gave me. ha ha. In case Bruno
didn't tell you when we were up to
their place we saw your room -
wedding pictures etc. You were adorable
Helen & Met was handsome. I know you
have a fine man for a hubby & visa
versa. Someday you'll drop in on us &
will show you our pictures etc too.
Okay.

Say if you want to send Met something
the 1st thing I'd say hed like is pictures
of you. If you can - get some film & send
it to him as somebody may have a
camera in his outfit. Write first & ask
if hed like some film & to state the size.
Pictures will live on & on. Don't you forget
that. Well Helen I'll close now - hoping to
see you in the near future. Your friend
Ange

18 THREE LETTERS FROM MY WIFE

June 19, 1945

Hello Fatstuff,

Just a few lines to let you know I was safe and sound in Bakersfield 7:15 p.m. & I could have made it sooner if I wanted to I went straight to the U.S.O. took a shower & shave & went skating. The rink opened at 8 p.m. It was hotter coming back than going up. Yes indeedy!!!

Monday morning I picked up my two day pass (which wasn't necessary) & went to the potato shed. While waiting for things to get started I changed my mind & worked for a carpenter for $1 an hour. I worked yesterday and today.

I received three letters from my wife today & she asked if I paid you a visit. She'll learn in due time. I'm enclosing her address in case you like to write to her.

I'm going to phone her tomorrow & I may take my furlough July 3rd.

I'll probably see Bruno & your in laws while I'm home & I'll tell them what a darling angel you are. (Pat yourself on the back.)

I'll tell them you're getting along fine & for them not to worry any. I'll tell my wife what happened while I was there as I didn't write much about it in my letter as I told her I'd tell here when I get home. I did mention a few things.

I'll write to Met in a day or so as I sent my last letter "free" & I never got an answer to it. I'll splurge and send it air mail. Ha ha. Oh wait til I tell him a few things. Am I going to pour it on thick. Your ears are going to burn plenty. Ha ha. You can take it out on me next time I come up. I'm going to wear a suit of armor, it will be your elbows that will hurt not my ribs. You'll be sorry now!

Well Helen I'm going to close now asking you to give everybody up there my regards & love. Tell them I said thanks for the swell time. I enjoyed myself. I hope I lived up to the build up Met gave me.

I'll close now hoping to hear from you in the near future.

Always, Your friend, Ange

June 19, 1945

Hello Fatstuff,

Just a few lines to let you know I was safe & sound in Bakersfield 7:15 P.M. & I could have made it sooner if I wanted to. I went straight to the U.S.O. took a shower & shave & went skating. The rink opened at 8 P.M. It was hotter coming back than going up. Yes indeedy!!!

Monday morning I picked up my two day pass (which wasn't necessary) & went to the potato shed. While waiting for things to get started I changed my mind & worked for a carpenter for $1 an hour. I worked yesterday & today.

I received three letters from

normal ways of living.

Glad to hear that math you a bracelet Helen out there. You cant buy gifts etc so you try a hand at making something in your spare time. If & when Med does send you more gifts you'll find what I said is true.

Between you & I Helen — I like California better than Jersey. This place is a paradise down here the weather is fine — plenty of jobs. Well its having your relatives back East etc that makes you want to go back. My parents are old & nearly helpless as far as speech & legal matters are concerned & somebody got to take care of them. But California is nice.

Helen I'll make that trip often pay day as I'll feel safe to travel. I have another wife to see in Alameda also. She staying there & waiting for her sailor husband to return. She's my Wifes best girlfriend. I'll write & let you know & I'll keep your telephone number handy too.

Are there nights you go out? I don't

I'm slated makes me drool. How I'd love to get back to my wife & be a civilian again. Well I can dream can't I? I was thinking of having her out here with me but I priced the rooms & its highway robbery $40 for 1 room — $60 for two. if you can find an opening. Well that will never do for me.

I'll wait another month & put in for a furlough. The reason I'm waiting is to see how large this next quota will be as I wish my next trip East is permanent. Period! So why throw $100 into the winds.

I'm glad you like the set up there — it makes things easier for you. Now if Mat was a sailor - his ship may get into port every so often but since he's not — well ———! Your guess is as good as mine. Taking when you staying helps a great deal too.

Well how long it will last now — who can say? I hope its short & sweet so we all can go home & back to our

want to miss you when I come up.
It will probably be over a week end
most likely. Sat. night or Sunday. I'll
let you know ahead of time for sure.

Hope Jean live up to the build up
Mel gave me. ha ha. In case Bruno
didn't tell you when we were up to
their place we saw your room -
wedding pictures etc. You were adorable
Helen & Mel was handsome. I know you
have a fine man for a hubby & visa
versa. Someday you'll drop in on us &
will show you our pictures etc too.
Okay.

Say if you want to send Mel something
the 1st thing I'd say he'd like is pictures
of you. If you can - get some film & send
it to him as somebody may have a
camera in his outfit. Write first & ask
if he'd like some film & to state the size.
Pictures will live on & on. Don't you forget
that. Well Helen I'll close now - hoping to
see you in the near future. Your friend
Ange

19 DISCHARGED AT LAST

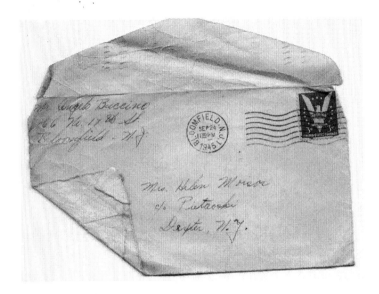

Sept. 24, 1945

Hello Helen,

Just a line to let you know I was discharged sat. I am now one happy civilian.

I'm running around like a chicken who's just had his head chopped off. Going to take things easy for a week or so then land a job.

Honest Helen I'm sorry I've delayed paying that debt but my mind is here & there – mostly there. At last I sat myself down & dood it. Enclosed you'll find five dollars.

I'll stop in and see Bruno as I'm going to live in my mother's house – ahem as soon as we can get those people out.

What's the latest from Met? Hope he's well. Better yet hope he comes home soon. Before Xmas I hope!!

Don't be scared to drop me a line once in a while Fatstuff or when Met gets home I'll have to start all over & greet you as a stranger.

How's things up there in Dexter? How's your mother? Better I hope.

Well Helen I'm running out of gab so I'll close trusting this letter finds you in the best of health. Give my regards to Met – by all means. Or else!!!

So long Fatstuff

Your friend, Ange.

Sept. 24, 1945

Hello Helen,

Just a line or two to let you know I was discharged Sat. I am now one happy Civilian.

I'm running around like a Chicken who's just had his head chopped off. Going to take things easy for a week or so then land a job.

Honest, Helen I'm sorry we delayed paying that debt but my mind is here & there — mostly there. At last I set myself down & did it. Enclosed you'll find five dollars.

I'll stop in & see Bruno as I'm going to live in my mothers house — whom as soon as we can get these people out.

Whats the latest from Mel? Hope
he's well. Better yet I hope he comes
home soon. Before Xmas I hope!!

Don't be scared to drop me a
line once in awhile Fatstuff or
when Mel gets home I'll have to start
all over & greet you as a stranger.

Hows things up there in Dexter?
Hows your Mother? Better I hope.
Well Helen I'm running out of gab
so I'll close trusting this little
finds you in the best of health.
Give my regards to Mel — by
all means. Or else...!!!

So long Fatstuff
Your friend.
George.

20 HOME FRONT

Lucy and Anthony Pavone at Gless Avenue

The Gless Avenue gang

Angelo, Marie and Val

Marie and Angelo

Pat Francisco, Julia and

Marie Cocozza, Angelo Buccino

Pat Francisco, Julia Cocozza, Angelo Buccino and Marie Cocozza

*Butch Depczek and future
sister-in-law Marie Cocozza*

Butch Depczek and Julia Cocozza
Future spouses

Mitch 'Met' aka 'Metalski' Mosior

Marie Cocozza challenges native gals

Near Army training facility in Virginia

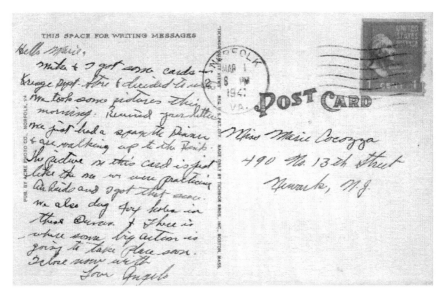

Near Army training facility in Virginia.

21 COLD WEATHER TRAINING

Artillery Training

Guard duty and a clean rifle

22 BAND OF BROTHERS

Battery B

Friends and buddies

23 IN THE TRENCHES

Somewhere in the South Pacific

24 FRIENDLY NATIVES

Whatever the natives traded, the tales did not make it stateside.

25 REST & RELAXATION

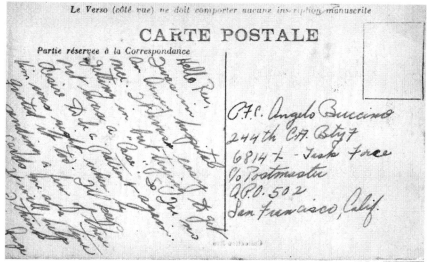

Noumea Hospital, New Calidonia

26 UNIT CITATIONS

THE SECRETARY OF THE NAVY

WASHINGTON

4 February 1943.

Cited in the Name of

The President of the United States

THE FIRST MARINE DIVISION, REINFORCED

Under command of

Major General Alexander A. Vandegrift, U.S.M.C.

CITATION:

"The officers and enlisted men of the First Marine Division, Reinforced, on August 7 to 9, 1942, demonstrated outstanding gallantry and determination in successfully executing forced landing assaults against a number of strongly defended Japanese positions on Tulagi, Gavutu, Tanambogo, Florida and Guadalcanal, British Solomon Islands, completely routing all the enemy forces and seizing a most valuable base and airfield within the enemy zone of operations in the South Pacific Ocean. From the above period until 9 December, 1942, this Reinforced Division not only held their important strategic positions despite determined and repeated Japanese naval, air and land attacks, but by a series of offensive operations against strong enemy resistance drove the Japanese from the proximity of the airfield and inflicted great losses on them by land and air attacks. The courage and determination displayed in these operations were of an inspiring order."

Frank Knox
Secretary of the Navy.

```
2350-75-10
DGP-hmg
```

DEC 26 1944

From: Director of Personnel, Marine Corps.
To: Private First Class Angelo Buccino, 32059032,
           U. S. Army, Company 19 - E.P.R.C. - Group
           1439, Camp Butner, North Carolina.
Via: The Commanding Officer.

Subject: Information concerning the Presidential Unit
           Citation ribbon bar.

Reference: (a) Your ltr. to the War Dept., dated 11-6-44
                forwarded to this office for reply.

1.   In reply to reference (a), information is
furnished that the Presidential Unit Citation ribbon
bar is worn by Naval personnel so entitled on the left
breast between personal decoration ribbons and service
medal ribbons. However, when medals are worn on the
uniform the Presidential Unit Citation insignia will
be worn on the right breast.

2.   War Department regulations authorize the
wearing of the above decoration by members of the Army
on the right breast at all times.

                             R. H. JESCHKE
- - - - - - - - - - - - - - - By direction - - - - - -

R E S T R I C T E D

HEADQUARTERS
AMERICAL DIVISION
APO 716

31 December 1943

GENERAL ORDERS)
  NO. 67   )   E X T R A C T

AWARDS OF THE PRESIDENTIAL UNIT CITATION

By direction of the President, and authority contained in paragraph
5, Letter, War Department, The Adjutant General's Office, AG 200.6 (29
Jul 43), subject: Eligibility of Army Personnel to the Presidential Unit
Citation and ribbon bar with star, dated 5 November 1943, and 1st Indorse-
ment, Headquarters USAFISPA, APO 502, AG 200.6 (7)1, dated 10 December 1943,
the Presidential Unit Citation is awarded to the following-named officers
and enlisted men of the Americal Division who served in actual combat with
the First Marine Division, Reinforced, on Guadalcanal at any time during the
period 7 August 1942 to 9 December 1942.

         *   *   *

        Pfc Angelo M Buccino 32059032
         *   *   *

By command of Major General HODGE:

                                   C. M. McQUARRIE
                                Colonel, General Staff Corps
OFFICIAL: Chief of Staff

        W. H. BIGGERSTAFF
Lieutenant Colonel, Adjutant General's Department
        Adjutant General

R E S T R I C T E D

27 WEDDING BELLS

Mr. and Mrs. Anthony Cocozza
request the honour of your presence
at the marriage of their daughter
Marie
to
Angelo Buccino
United States Army
son of
Mr. and Mrs. Carmine Pavone
on Tuesday, the twenty-fourth of October
Nineteen hundred and forty-four
at five-thirty o'clock
Saint Francis Church
North Seventh Street and Abington Avenue
Newark, New Jersey

Reception at 7:30 o'clock
466 North 17th Street
Bloomfield, New Jersey

28 HONORABLE DISCHARGE

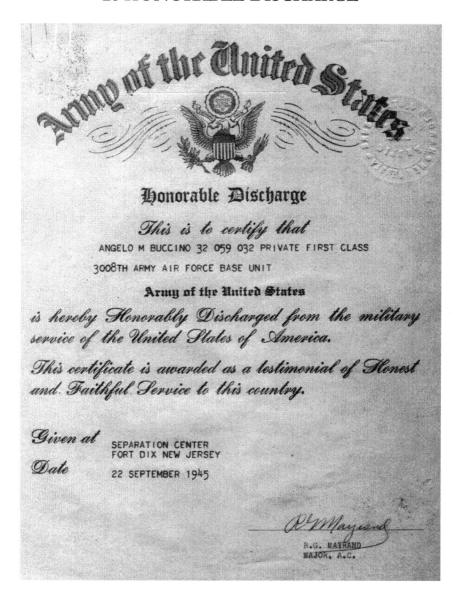

ENLISTED RECORD AND REPORT OF SEPARATION
HONORABLE DISCHARGE

1. LAST NAME - FIRST NAME - MIDDLE INITIAL	2. ARMY SERIAL NO.	3. GRADE	4. ARM OR SERVICE	5. COMPONENT
BUCCINO ANGELO M	32 059 032	PFC	AAF	AUS

6. ORGANIZATION	7. DATE OF SEPARATION	8. PLACE OF SEPARATION
3008TH AAF BU	22 SEP 45	SEP CNTR FT DIX NJ

9. PERMANENT ADDRESS FOR MAILING PURPOSES	10. DATE OF BIRTH	11. PLACE OF BIRTH
86 GLESS AVE BELLEVILLE NJ	16 NOV 18	NUTLEY NJ

12. ADDRESS FROM WHICH EMPLOYMENT WILL BE SOUGHT	13. COLOR EYES	14. COLOR HAIR	15. HEIGHT	16. WEIGHT	17. NO. DEPEND.
SEE 9	GREY	BR	5-4½	155 lbs	2

18. RACE	19. MARITAL STATUS	20. U.S. CITIZEN	21. CIVILIAN OCCUPATION AND NO.
W	X	X	FEEDER II 8-70.01

MILITARY HISTORY

22. DATE OF INDUCTION	23. DATE OF ENLISTMENT	24. DATE OF ENTRY INTO ACTIVE SERVICE	25. PLACE OF ENTRY INTO SERVICE
7 FEB 41		7 FEB 41	NEWARK NJ

26. SELECTIVE SERVICE DATA	27. REGISTERED	27. LOCAL S.S. BOARD NO.	28. COUNTY AND STATE	29. HOME ADDRESS AT TIME OF ENTRY INTO SERVICE
	X	9	ESSEX NJ	SEE 9

30. MILITARY OCCUPATIONAL SPECIALTY AND NO.	31. MILITARY QUALIFICATION AND DATE
GUN CREWMAN LIGHT ARTILLERY 844	EXP GUNNER GO 86 HQ 244 CA 7 AUG 41

32. BATTLES AND CAMPAIGNS
NORTHERN SOLOMONS   GO 33 WD 45 AS AMENDED

33. DECORATIONS AND CITATIONS DISTINGUISHED UNIT BADGE GOOD CONDUCT MEDAL ASIATIC-PACIFIC SERVICE MEDAL

34. WOUNDS RECEIVED IN ACTION
NONE

35. LATEST IMMUNIZATION DATES				36. SERVICE OUTSIDE CONTINENTAL U.S. AND RETURN		
SMALLPOX	TYPHOID	TETANUS	OTHER (specify)	DATE OF DEPARTURE	DESTINATION	DATE OF ARRIVAL
26 JUN 44	10 FEB 45	4 JUN 44	NONE	23 JAN 42	WPTO	12 MAR 42
				13 SEP 44	USA	3 OCT 44

37. TOTAL LENGTH OF SERVICE				38. HIGHEST GRADE HELD
CONTINENTAL SERVICE		FOREIGN SERVICE		
YEARS	MONTHS	DAYS	YEARS	MONTHS	DAYS	
1	10	8	2	9	8	PFC

39. PRIOR SERVICE
NONE

40. REASON AND AUTHORITY FOR SEPARATION CONVENIENCE OF THE GOVERNMENT AR 615-365 15 DEC 1944 & RR 1-1 (DEMOBILIZATION) AS AMENDED BY TWX TAG 4 SEP 45

41. SERVICE SCHOOLS ATTENDED	42. EDUCATION (Years)		
NONE	Grammar 8	High School 3	College 0

PAY DATA

43. LONGEVITY FOR PAY PURPOSES		44. MUSTERING OUT PAY	45. SOLDIER DEPOSITS	46. TRAVEL PAY	47. TOTAL AMOUNT, NAME OF DISBURSING OFFICER
YEARS 4	MONTHS 7	TOTAL 300	THIS PMT 100	NONE	260 H M FIX MAJFD

INSURANCE NOTICE

48. KIND OF INSURANCE	49. HOW PAID	50. Effective Date of Allot.	51. Date of Next Premium Due	52. PREMIUM DUE EACH MONTH	53. INTENTION OF VETERAN TO
X	X	30 SEP 45	31 OCT 45	3.30	X

54. REMARKS (This space for completion of above items or entry of other items specified in W.D. Directives)
LAPEL BUTTON ISSUED ASR SCORE (2 SEP 45) 92

56. SIGNATURE OF PERSON BEING SEPARATED	57. PERSONNEL OFFICER (Type name, grade and organization - signature)
Angelo M. Buccino	E J MATHEWS 1ST LT QM E.J. Mathews

National World War Two Museum, New Orleans, La.

131

ABOUT THE AUTHOR

Angelo Buccino was born on Columbia Avenue in Nutley. He grew up on Gless Avenue in Belleville on the Nutley/Belleville border. He lived next door to his best friend Mitch Mosior. Angelo was drafted in 1941, he served on a gun crew, light artillery, in the Solomons with Marines First Division and AmeriCal. While overseas, he wrote to his best friend when he could.

Prior to the service, he met Marie Cocozza while roller skating at Branch Brook Park in Newark. They married in Newark on October 24, 1944. They had three children, Lucille, Marie, and Anthony, and four grand-children.

Mitch and Helen Mosior lived in Nutley for six decades and were best friends of Angelo and Marie. The men shared their love of racing pigeons and the women shared their love of bingo. Angelo was Godfather to Mitch's daughter Mary Ellen. Mitch was Godfather to Angelo's son Anthony.

Made in the USA
Middletown, DE
23 August 2019